BEDFORD

BROMHAM, KEMPSTON, SANDY

Cardington, Clapham, Cople, Great Barford, Pavenham, Renhold, Stewartby, Willington, Wilstead, Wootton

2nd edition July 2003

Original edition printed May 2001

Published by AA Publishing (a trading name of Automobile Association Developments Limited, whose registered office is Millstream, Maidenhead Road, Windsor, Berkshire SL4 5GD. Registered number 1878835).

Mapping produced by the Cartography Department of The Automobile Association. (A01718)

A CIP Catalogue record for this book is available from the British Library.

Printed by GRAFIASA S.A., Porto, Portugal

Ref: ML106z

Key to map pages ii-iii

Key to map symbols iv–1

Enlarged map pages 2-3

Main map pages 4-43

Index – towns & villages 44

Index – streets 45-49

Index – featured places 49-50

Acknowledgements 50

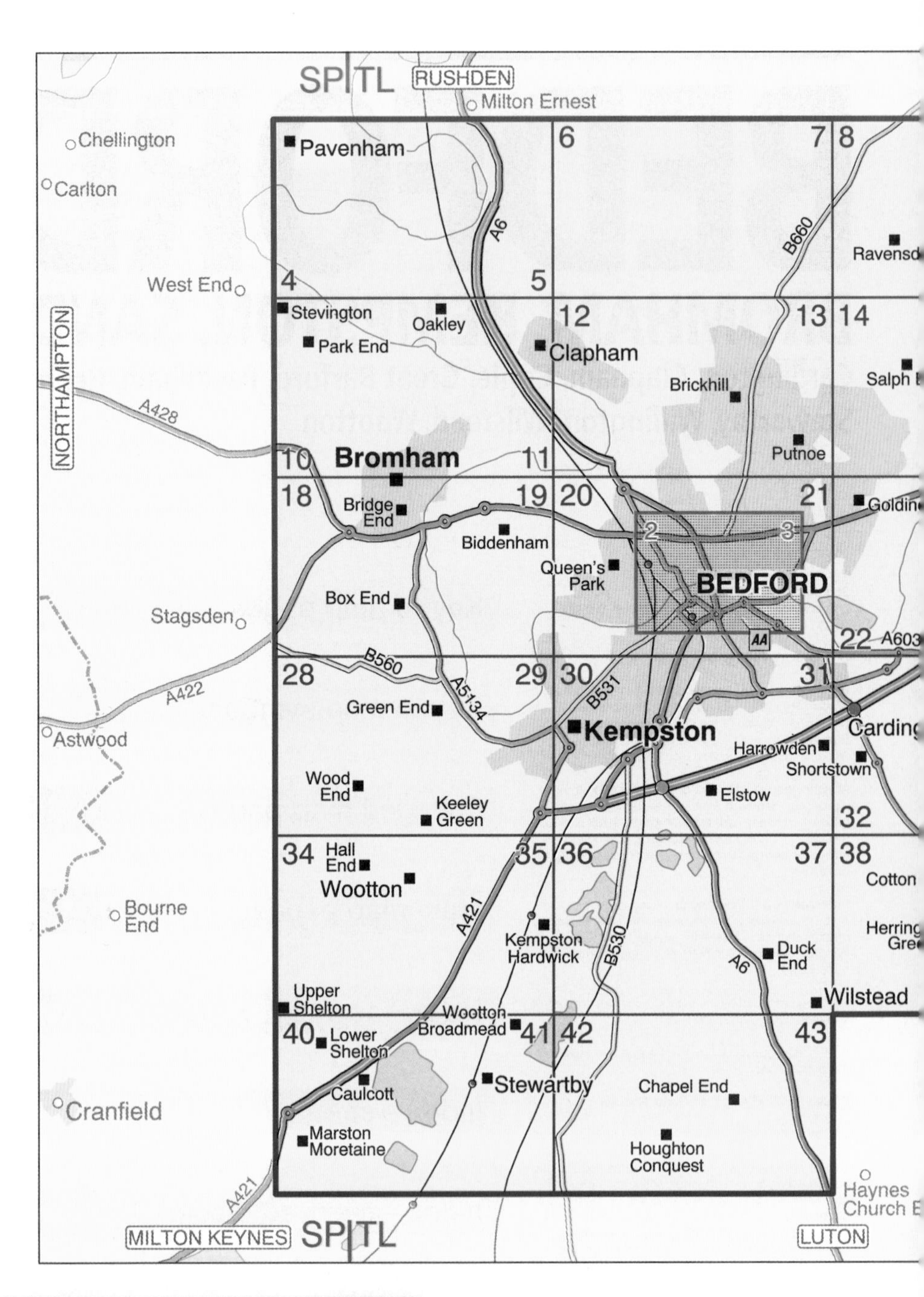

6.3 inches to 1 mile

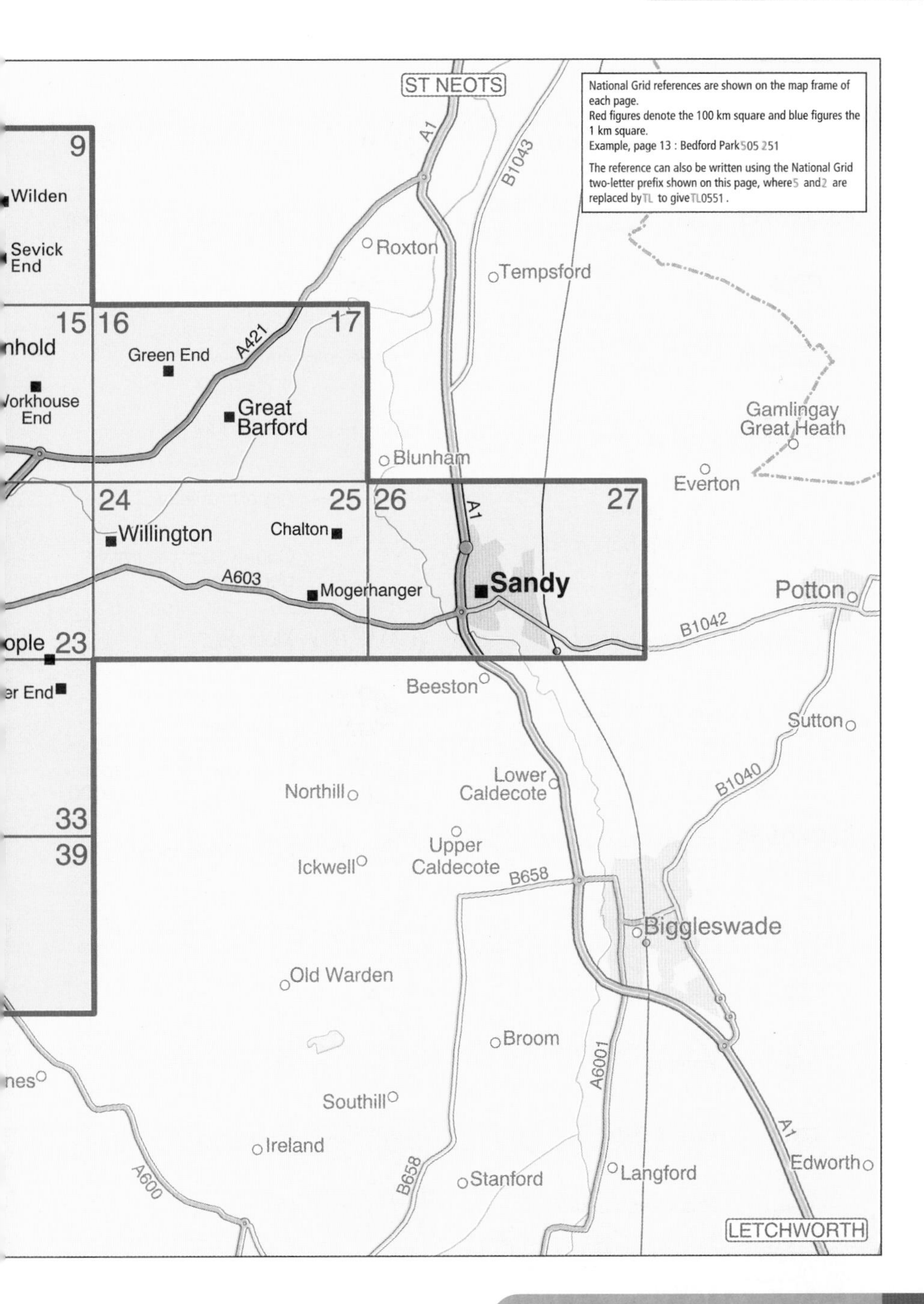

4.2 inches to 1 mile **Scale of main map pages** **1:15,000**

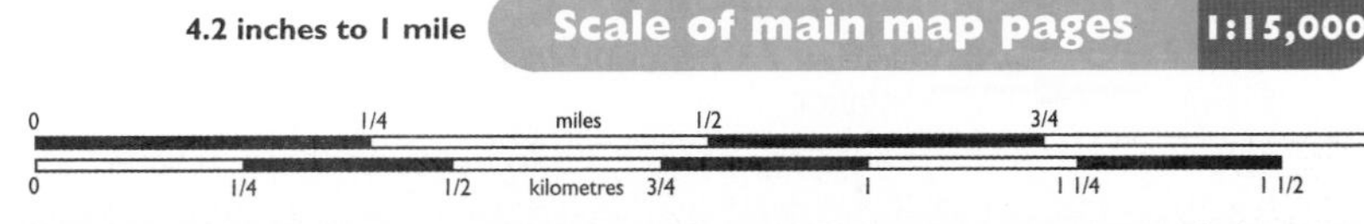

Junction 9 — Motorway & junction

Services — Motorway service area

Primary road single/dual carriageway

Services — Primary road service area

A road single/dual carriageway

B road single/dual carriageway

Other road single/dual carriageway

Minor/private road, access may be restricted

One-way street

Pedestrian area

Track or footpath

Road under construction

Road tunnel

AA — AA Service Centre

P — Parking

P+ — Park & Ride

Bus/coach station

Railway & main railway station

Railway & minor railway station

Underground station

Light railway & station

Preserved private railway

LC — Level crossing

Tramway

Ferry route

Airport runway

County, administrative boundary

Mounds

17 — Page continuation 1:15,000

3 — Page continuation to enlarged scale 1:10,000

River/canal, lake

Aqueduct, lock, weir

465 Winter Hill — Peak (with height in metres)

Beach

Woodland

Park

Cemetery

Built-up area

Symbol	Meaning	Symbol	Meaning
	Featured building		Abbey, cathedral or priory
	City wall		Castle
A&E	Hospital with 24-hour A&E department		Historic house or building
PO	Post Office	Wakehurst Place NT	National Trust property
	Public library		Museum or art gallery
	Tourist Information Centre		Roman antiquity
	Seasonal Tourist Information Centre		Ancient site, battlefield or monument
	Petrol station, 24-hour Major suppliers only		Industrial interest
	Church/chapel		Garden
	Public toilets		Garden Centre Garden Centre Association Member
	Toilet with disabled facilities		Garden Centre Wyevale Garden Centre
PH	Public house AA recommended		Farm or animal centre
	Restaurant AA inspected		Zoological or wildlife collection
Madeira Hotel	Hotel AA inspected		Bird collection
	Theatre or performing arts centre		Nature reserve
	Cinema		Aquarium
	Golf course		Visitor or heritage centre
	Camping AA inspected		Country park
	Caravan site AA inspected		Cave
	Camping & caravan site AA inspected		Windmill
	Theme park		Distillery, brewery or vineyard

BEDFORD
MK40
1 grid square represents 250 metres
Rushmoor School
Livingstone Lower School
Robinson Pool
Surgery
Polam School
Harper Music School
University
Bowen West Theatre
Union Street Clinic
Marlowes Health Centre
De Parys Medical Centre
Bedford High Sch
HM Prison
Bedford Preparatory School
St Bedes Middle Sch
Priory Lower Sch
Bus Station
Police Stn
Church Arcade
The Arcade
Corn Exchange
Harpur Centre
Bedford Station
Civic Theatre
Town Hall
Bedford Magistrates Court
Star Rowing Club
County Hall
Bedford College of Further Education
Sikh Temple
Bedford St Johns Station
Bedford Hospital
St Johns Special School
Cauldwell
SHAKESPEARE ROAD
A5141
BROMHAM ROAD
ASHBURNHAM ROAD
UNION STREET
TAVISTOCK STREET
A6
GREYFRIARS
DAME ALICE STREET
HIGH STREET
ST PETER'S
A428
THE BROADWAY
RIVER STREET
HORNE LANE
ST PAUL'S SQ
ST MARY'S STREET
CAULDWELL STREET
ST JOHN'S STREET
KINGSWAY
PREBEND STREET
BRITANNIA ROAD
KEMPSTON ROAD
B531
MIDLAND RD
Ford End Road
Ouse

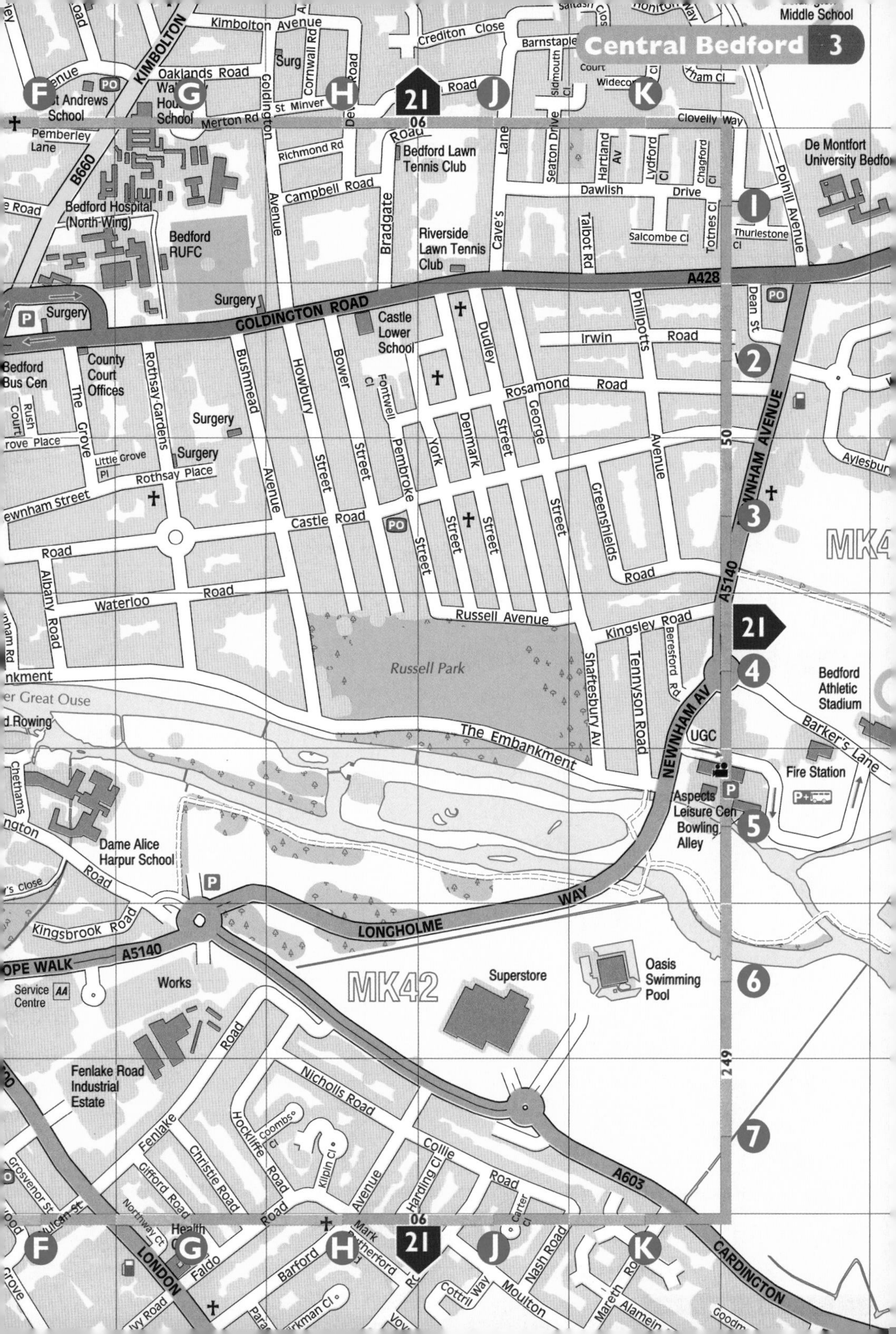
Kimbolton Avenue
Crediton Close
Barnstaple
Middle School
Oaklands Road
KIMBOLTON
Goldington
Cornwall Rd
Surg
St Andrews School
St Minver
Merton Rd
Clovelly Way
Pemberley Lane
B660
Richmond Rd
Bedford Lawn Tennis Club
Campbell Road
Bradgate
Lane
Caves
Seaton Drive
Hartland Av
Lydford Cl
Chagford Cl
Dawlish
Drive
De Montfort University Bedford
Polhill Avenue
Bedford Hospital (North Wing)
Bedford RUFC
Riverside Lawn Tennis Club
Talbot Rd
Salcombe Cl
Totnes Cl
Thurlestone Cl
A428
GOLDINGTON ROAD
Surgery
Castle Lower School
Dudley
Philpotts
Dean St
Irwin
Road
Bedford Bus Cen
County Court Offices
Rothsay Gardens
Bushmead Avenue
Howbury Street
Bower Street
Fontwell Cl
Rosamond
Road
George Street
NEWNHAM AVENUE
Rush Court
The Grove
Surgery
Pembroke Street
York
Denmark Street
Little Grove Pl
Rothsay Place
Avenue
Aylesbury
Newnham Street
Castle Road
PO
Greenshields
MK4
Road
Albany Road
Waterloo
Road
Russell Avenue
A5140
21
Kingsley Road
Beresford Rd
Tennyson Road
Shaftesbury Av
Russell Park
Embankment
River Great Ouse
Rowing
The Embankment
NEWNHAM AV
UGC
Bedford Athletic Stadium
Barker's Lane
Fire Station
Chethams
Aspects Leisure Cen
Bowling Alley
Dame Alice Harpur School
Road
Kingsbrook Road
LONGHOLME
WAY
A5140
HOPE WALK
Service Centre
Works
MK42
Superstore
Oasis Swimming Pool
Fenlake Road Industrial Estate
Road
Nicholls Road
Hockliffe Road
Coombs Cl
Kilpin Cl
Fenlake
Christie Road
Gifford Road
Collie
Road
A603
Grosvenor St
Vulcan St
Northway Cl
Avenue
Harding Cl
Carter Cl
Health Centre
Faldo
LONDON
Barford
Mark Rutherford
Nash Road
Cottril Way
Moulton
Mareth Rd
Alamein
CARDINGTON
Goodm
Ivy Road
Parkman Cl
06
50
249

4
A
B
C
D
Golf Course
499
500
56
55
254
1
2
3
4
5
Church Lane
Pavenham
Pavenham Park Golf Course
Brookfields Cl
Weavers Lane
Pavenham Road
John Bunyan Trail
Close Rd
Mill Lane
Mill
Westfields Farm
Westfield Road
River Great Ouse
Bunyan Trail
Stafford Bridge
Oakley
Queens Cl
Town Farm
Church Road
Stevington
Dewlands
10
1 grid square represents 500 metres

Ernest
RUSHDEN ROAD
Huntsmans Way
Arkwright Rd
Riverside Vw
PO
River Lane
End
London
Marsh La
Starey Cl
Church Close
Church
Thurleigh Road
Milton Ernest Lower School
Parkside
Church Gn
02
03
56
55
254
E
F
G
H
I
2
3
4
5
6
11
BEDFORD ROAD
Milton House
The Grange
East End Farm
A6
Highfield Road
Judges Spinney
Milton Road
Clapham Hospital
Station Road
Lincroft
Reynes Dr
Brckwll
Cpthrn
Pth
Hunts
Lincroft Middle School
Tinsley Cl
Twinwood Rd
Bridle Dr
Paddock Cl
Sd Cl
Duke Dr
Knights Ave
John Bunyan Tr
Clapham

A
B
C
D
503
04
56
55
254
1
2
3
4
5
Outfields Farm
Twinwood Farm
Twin Wood
The Baulk
Green Lane
12
Clapham
1 grid square represents 500 metres
Avenue

E
F
G
H
06
07
56
55
254
I
2
3
4
5
8
13
Wood End
Ravensden House
SUNDERLAND HILL
Grange Farm
Thurleigh Road
Graze Hill
Graze Hill House
Butler Street
S Cl
PO
New Cl
B660
Oldways Road
BEDFORD ROAD
Cleat Hill
Hom
Farm
Churnet Cl
Westrope Way
Test Cl
Road
Mowsbury

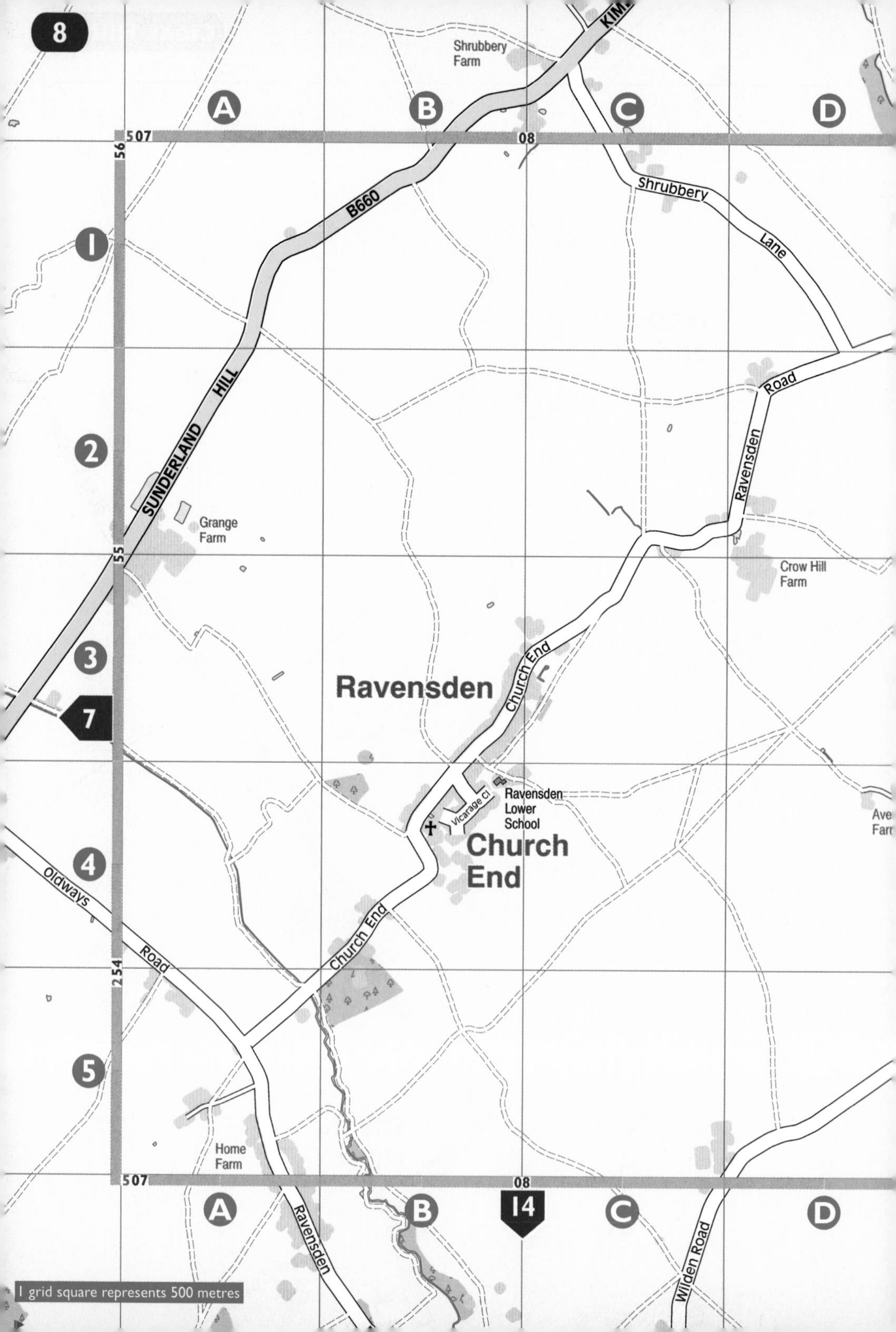
Shrubbery Farm
A
B
C
D
507
08
56
B660
Shrubbery
Lane
1
Road
SUNDERLAND
HILL
2
Ravensden
Grange Farm
55
Crow Hill Farm
3
Church End
Ravensden
7
Ravensden Lower School
Vicarage Cl
Church End
4
Oldways
Church End
Road
254
5
Home Farm
507
08
A
B
14
C
D
Ravensden
Wilden Road
1 grid square represents 500 metres

Wilden Gallery
Rectory Farm
E
F
G
H
10
11
Duck's Cross
56
I
Chequers Hill
Colesden Road
East End Lane
2
Wilden
High Street
Manor Cl
Wilden VA Lower School
East End
Hollis Lane
55
3
Sevick End
4
Barford Road
254
5
Northfield Farm
15
Great Early Grove

10
Great Ouse
Trail
Stevington
Park End
Church Road
Burridge's Cl
The Bakery
Farley Way
Foxbrook
Silver Street
PO
Park Road
Mill Farm
Post Mill
John Bunyan Trail
Westfield Road
Queens Cl
Town Farm
Dewlands
Oakley House
Church
Park Road
BROMHAM
Wood
Wing
Molivers Lane
Tudor Close
Mowbray Cl
Cornwallis Close
Springfield Dr
Bromham VC Lower School
Grange Lane
The Glade
Red Cedar Rd
Chestnut Av
Stone Pine Rd
Tulip Tree Cl
Rainbow Special Sch
Parkland
Chestnut Avenue
Northampton Road
ROAD
Bromham Grange
Neville Crs
Godwin Cl
Godwin Wy
Trevor Drive
Rosemary Drive
Brook Way
Webbs Cl
Ley Side
Bucks Cl
A428
1 grid square represents 500 metres
A
B
C
D
1
2
3
4
5
4
18
499
500
53
52
251

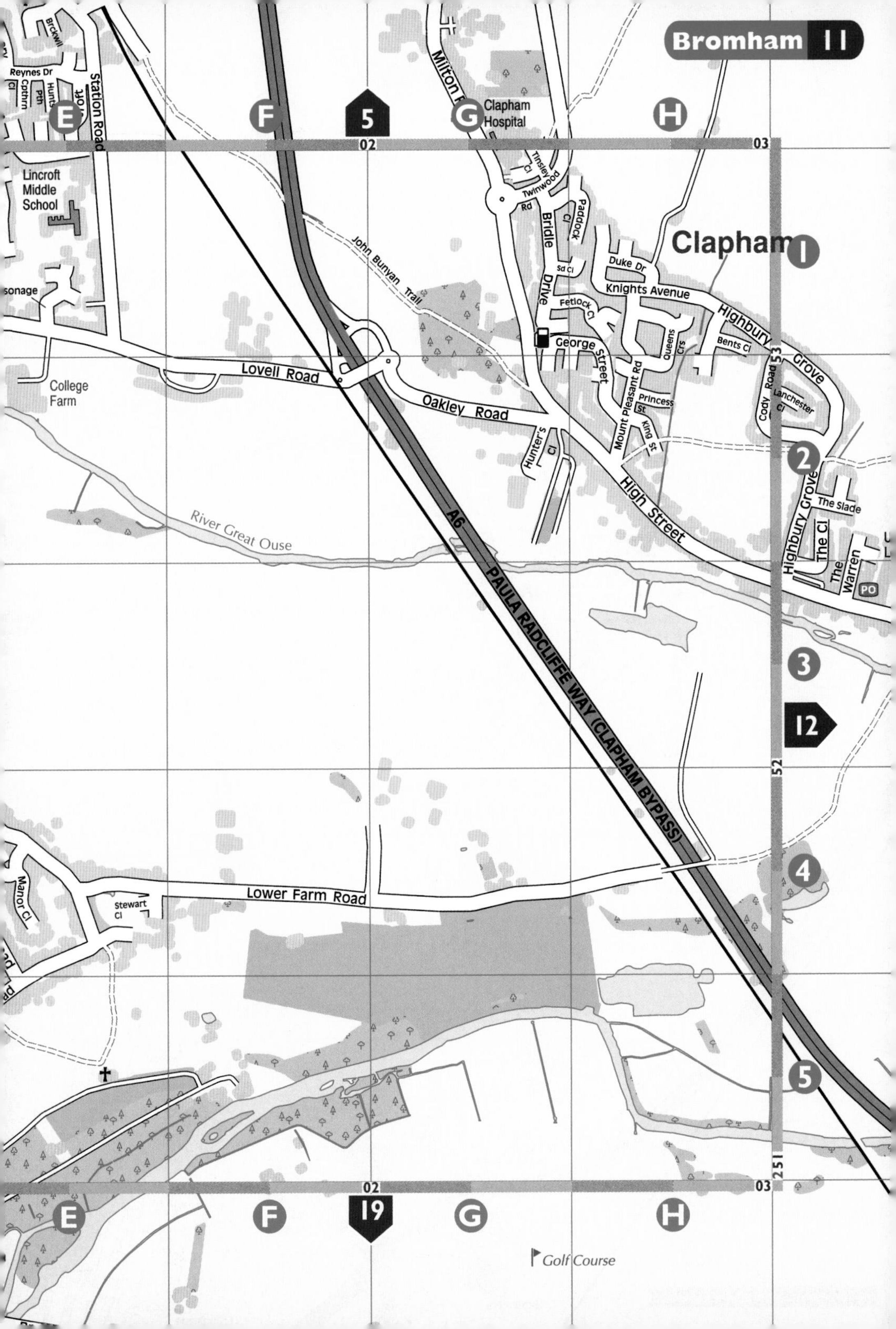

Clapham
Clapham Hospital
Lincroft Middle School
College Farm
Station Road
Reynes Dr
Milton Rd
Tinsley Cl
Twinwood Rd
Bridle Drive
Paddock Cl
Duke Dr
Knights Avenue
Highbury Grove
Bents Cl
Cody Road
Lanchester Cl
Fetlock Cl
Sd Cl
George Street
Queens Crs
Mount Pleasant Rd
Princess St
King St
Hunter's Cl
High Street
The Slade
The Cl
The Warren
PO
John Bunyan Trail
Lovell Road
Oakley Road
River Great Ouse
A6
PAULA RADCLIFFE WAY (CLAPHAM BYPASS)
Lower Farm Road
Stewart Cl
Manor Cl
Golf Course
sonage

5
12
19

12
A
B
6
C
D
Green Lane
503
04
Clapham
Avenue
Highbury Grove
Queens Crs
Bents Cl
Cody Road
Lanchester Cl
Green Lane
Bedford & County Golf Club
Golf Course
Clapham Park
Carriage Drive
John Bunyan Trail
Hawk Drive
Highbury Grove
The Slade
The Cl
The Warren
Street
Ursula Taylor Lower School
Ursula Taylor Wk
PO
Church Vw
Clapham Green
Woodlands Manor Hotel
Bedford Road
Green Lane
Woodlands Park
John Bunyan Trail
Beauch Middle
11
52
53
Curlew Crescent
Plover Way
Industrial Estate
Murdock Road
Works
Clapham Road
River Great Ouse
Manton Lane
Brickhill Drive
Eagle Gardens
John Bunyan Trail
Cemetery
Lely Close
Cotman Cl
Gainsborough Rise
Wedgwood Road
Rowlandson Wy
Haden Cl
Ramsay Cl
Kneller Cl
Turner Way
Bedford Modern School
SOUTH ROUNDABOUT
251
503
04
A
B
C
D
20
Cut Throat
A6
Manton Lane
Lower School
Constable Hl
Hogarth Cl
Landseer Walk
Slade Walk
Park Road North
Gladstone Street
Hartington Street
Sedgemoor College
MANTON LANE ROUNDABOUT
Superstore
Byron Crs
Stanley Street
Livingstone
1 grid square represents 500 metres

Cleat Hill
Mowsbury Golf Club
Golf Course
MK41
Mowsbury Park
Bedford Athletic RUFC
Brickhill
Brickhill Lower School
Bedford College
Bedford Park
Putnoe
The Hills Lower Sch
Hazeldene Lower School
Putnoe Lower School
Newnham Middle School
St John Rigby Lower School
Goldington Middle School
Wood
CLEAT HILL
KIMBOLTON ROAD
B660
Tyne Crescent
Douglas Road
Hamble Road
Bourneside
Avon Dr
Falcon Avenue
Brickhill Drive
Fulmar Road
Larkway
Pipit Rise
Aspen Avenue
Poplar Avenue
Harrington Dr
Rowallan Dr
Pax Hill
Brecon Way
Putnoe Lane
Queen's Drive
Woodcote Way
Stancliffe Road
Chiltern Avenue
Ellis Road
Pennine Rd
Wentworth
Windrush Avenue
Waveney Av
Waveney Avenue
Humber Av
Severn Way
Conway Crs
Torridge Ri
Wansbeck Rd
Carron Rd
Beaufort Way
Moriston Rd
Clyde Crs
Trent Rd
Birkdale Road
Foxlease
Wagstaffe Cl
Glenrose Av
Parkstone Cl
Prinknash Rd
Newstead Way
Buckfast Av
Fountains Rd
Pershore Cl
Heronscroft
Haylands
Mendip Crs
Selsey Avenue
Polhill Ave
Malvern Av
Brookfield Rd
Portland Close
Purbeck Close
Roundmead
Surgery
Surg
St Augustine's Road
St Michael's Road
St Andrews Rd
Pemberley
Balmoral Av
Kimbolton Avenue
The Acorn School
PO
E F G H
1 2 3 4 5
7
14
21
06
07
51 52 53

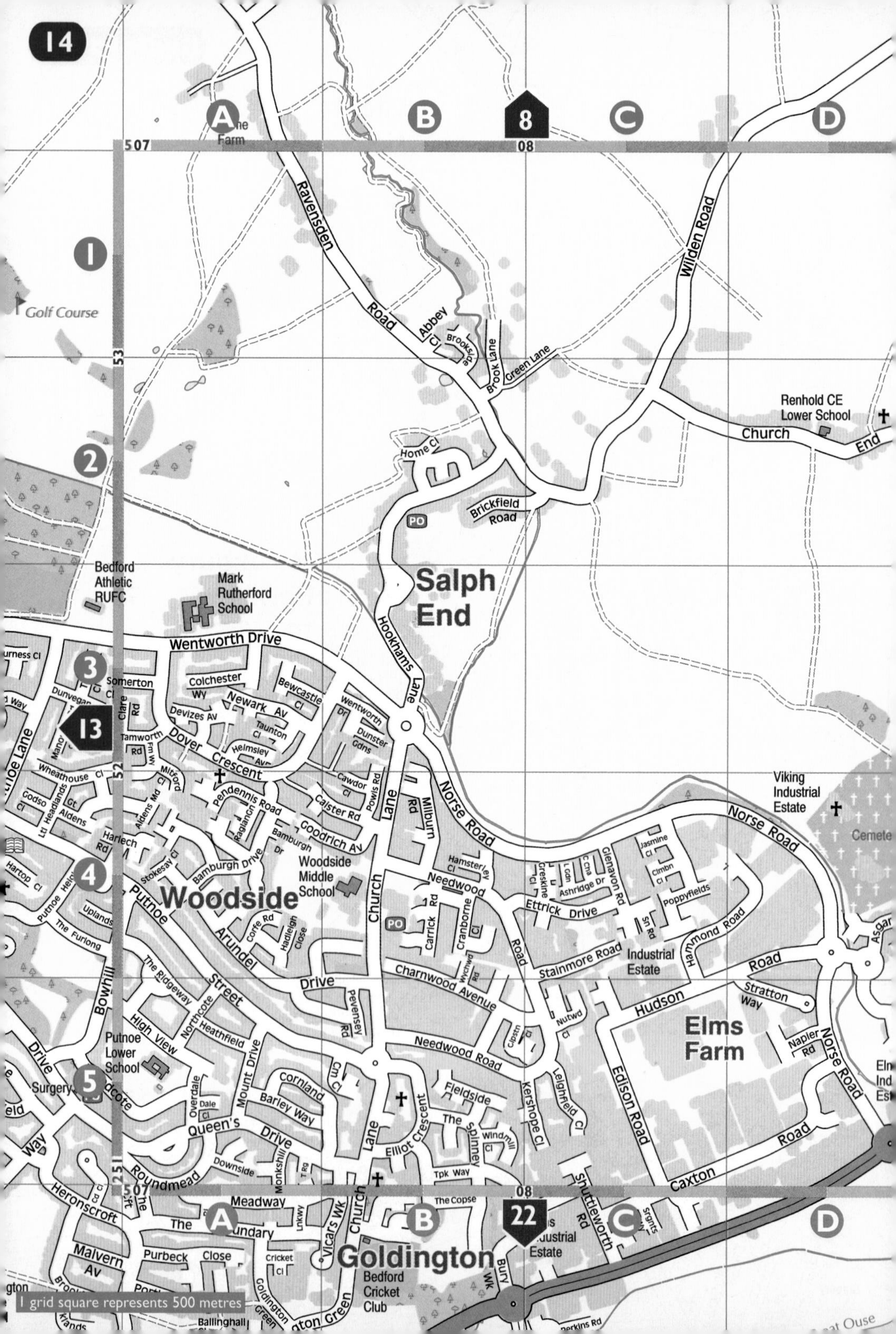

A
B
C
D
8
507
08
1
2
3
4
5
53
52
51
13
22
Golf Course
Ravensden Road
Abbey Cl
Brookside
Brook Lane
Green Lane
Wilden Road
Renhold CE Lower School
Church End
Home Cl
Brickfield Road
PO
Salph End
Bedford Athletic RUFC
Mark Rutherford School
Hookhams Lane
Wentworth Drive
Somerton
Colchester Wy
Newark Av
Bewcastle Cl
Wentworth Dr
Dunster Gdns
Devizes Av
Taunton Cl
Helmsley Av
Dover Crescent
Tamworth Rd
Clare Rd
Dunvegan
Mitford
Pendennis Road
Cawdor Cl
Powis Rd
Caister Rd
Goodrich Av
Bamburgh Dr
Norse Road
Milburn Rd
Lane
Viking Industrial Estate
Wheathouse Cl
Godso
Aldens
Headlands
Harlech Rd
Aldens Md
Stokesay Cl
Bamburgh Drive
Woodside Middle School
Hamsterley Cl
Needwood
Greskine Cl
Ashridge Dr
Glenavon Rd
Jasmine Cl
Poppyfields
Woodside
Hartop Cl
Putnoe
Uplands
The Furlong
Corfe Rd
Hadleigh Close
Arundel
Church
PO
Carrick Rd
Cranborne Cl
Ettrick Drive
Road
Stainmore Road
Industrial Estate
Hammond Road
Road
Bowhill
The Ridgeway
Street
Drive
Charnwood Avenue
Pevensey Rd
Hudson
Stratton Way
High View
Northcote
Heathfield
Mount Drive
Needwood Road
Nutwd Cl
Elms Farm
Napier Rd
Putnoe Lower School
Surgery
Overdale
Dale Cl
Cornland
Barley Way
Cm Cl
Fieldside
Kershope Cl
Leighfield Cl
Edison Road
Queen's Drive
The Spinney
Windmill Cl
Elliot Crescent
Road
Roundmead
Downside
Monkshill
Tpk Way
Caxton
Shuttleworth Rd
Heronscroft
Meadway
The Boundary
Lnkwy
Vicars Wk
The Copse
Malvern Av
Purbeck Close
Cricket Cl
Goldington
Bedford Cricket Club
Bury Wk
Estate
Goldington Green
Ballinghall
Perkins Rd
1 grid square represents 500 metres

Northfield Farm
E
F
9
G
H
10
11
I
Great Early Grove
Wood Lane
The Creakers
53
Woodfield Farm
Top End
2
enhold
Woodfield Lane
Green End
Workhouse End
Becher Cl
Becher Cl
3
Brewe Farm
16
52
Water End
Howbury Hall
4
A428 ST NEOTS ROAD
ST NEOTS ROAD
5
251
10
11
E
F
23
G
H

16
Northfield Farm
A
B
C
D
Birchfield Road
Barford Road
Green End
Green End Road
Fishers Cl
Peashill Lane
Penwrights La
Chapel Fld
Dothans Cl
Chapel Cl
Coopers Cl
Bd Rd
PO
Hunts Fl
Pyms
Silver St
Bereford Close
Great Barfo
Lower Scho
Brewer's Hall Farm
15
BEDFORD ROAD
A421
ST NEOTS ROAD
24
1
2
3
4
5
1 grid square represents 500 metres

E
F
G
H
14
15
A421
Great Barford House
ROXTON
ROAD
A421
River Great Ouse
I
53
2
3
52
4
5
51
Addingtons Road
New Road
Great Barford
The Cl
Saville Cl
School Lane
Street
Churchgate
Orchard Way
Barford Road
Blunham Grange
Grange Road
Pound Cl
Blunham
Brickh Close
Walnut Cl
The Hill
PO
Park Lane
Park Vw
The Avenue
Station
Cemetery
25

Rainbow Special Sch
Chestnut Avenue
Parkland
Northampton Road
Bromham VC Lower School
Springfield Dr
Close
Cornwallis
Grange Lane
10
A
B
C
D
499
500
51
50
249
Neville Crs
Godwin Cl
Godwin Wy
Randalls Cl
John Bunyan Trail
Bromham Grange
Northampton Road
Trevor Drive
Rosemary Drive
Brook Way
Webbs Cl
Ley Side
Bucks Cl
Berry Drive
Dynevor Cl
Princes Road
Stagsden Road
Dovehouse Cl
Tollgate Cl
Jackman Cl
Thistley Lane
Mayhew Cl
Quenby Wy
Brett Drive
Symonds Cl
A5134
A428
Walnut Cl
Partridge Lane
Pear Tree Close
Lime Cl
New Road
Quenby Way
BOX END ROAD
Works
Stagsden Road
A422
Wickend Farm
Dropshort Farm
Moorland
1
2
3
4
5
Road
Hanger Wood
John Bunyan Trail
Cross
Foss
BOX
Box End
West End Road
B560
SPRING LANE
28
Astey Wood
1 grid square represents 500 metres

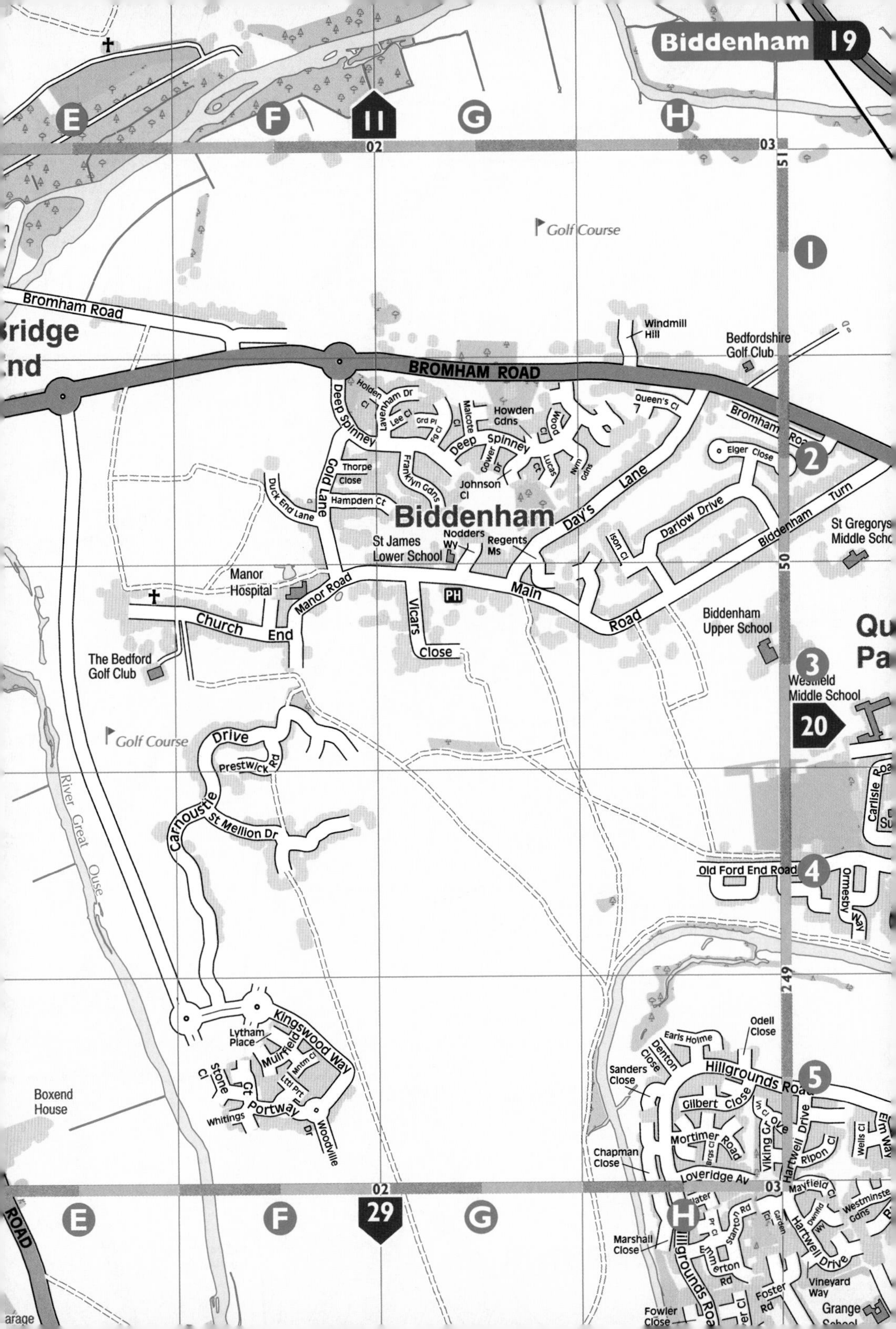

Biddenham
Bromham Road
BROMHAM ROAD
Bridge End
Golf Course
Windmill Hill
Bedfordshire Golf Club
Holden Cl
Lavenham Dr
Lee Cl
Grd Pl
Fg Cl
Malcote Cl
Howden Gdns
Wood Cl
Queen's Cl
Deep Spinney
Gold Lane
Thorpe Close
Franklyn Gdns
Gower Dr
Lucas Ct
Nvm Gdns
Johnson Cl
Elger Close
Day's Lane
Duck End Lane
Hampden Ct
Darlow Drive
Biddenham Turn
St Gregorys Middle Sch
St James Lower School
Nodders Wy
Regents Ms
Ison Cl
Manor Hospital
Manor Road
Main Road
PH
Vicars Close
Church End
The Bedford Golf Club
Biddenham Upper School
Westfield Middle School
Drive
Prestwick Rd
Carnoustie
St Mellion Dr
River Great Ouse
Carlisle Road
Old Ford End Road
Ormesby Way
Kingswood Way
Lytham Place
Muirfield
Stone Cl
Ct
Portway
Whitings
Woodville Dr
Boxend House
Odell Close
Earls Holme
Denton Close
Sanders Close
Hillgrounds Road
Gilbert Close
Mortimer Road
Viking Grove
Hartwell Drive
Ripon Cl
Wells Cl
Elm Way
Chapman Close
Loveridge Av
Mayfield Cl
Westminster Gdns
Marshall Close
Stanton Rd
Emmerton Rd
Foster Rd
Vineyard Way
Grange School
Fowler Close
Hillgrounds Road
ROAD
E F G H I
2 3 4 5
02 03 50 51 249
11 20 29

20
A
B
C
D
12
19
30
I
2
3
4
5
503
04
51
50
249
Bedford Modern School
SOUTH ROUNDABOUT
Cut Throat La
A6
Sedgemoor College
Superstore
MANTON LANE ROUNDABOUT
Manton Lane
Edith Cavell Lower School
Brickhill
Lely close
Cotman Cl
Rowlandson
Haden Cl
Gainsborough Rise
Ramsay Cl
Wedgwood Road
John Bunyan Trail
Cemetery
Kneller Cl
Turner Way
Constable Hl
Hogarth Cl
Landseer Walk
Slade Walk
Park Road North
Gladstone Street
Hartington Street
Salisbury Street
Stanley Street
Livingstone Lower School
Palmerston St
Beaconsfield
Garfield St
Pk Rd W
School
Roff Avenue
Byron Crs
Keats Cl
Sch
SHAKESPEARE ROAD
A5141
Cowper Road
Sidney Road
Spenser Road
Chaucer Road
Milton Road
Surg
Warwick Ave
Linden Rd
De Montfort University
Lansdowne Rd
Tudor Cl
Bowen West Thtr
Union Street Clnc
UNION STREET
Surgery
Trevor St
The Crescent
Boswell Court
Queen St
Works
Marlowes Hlth Cen
Chandos
Cavendish St
Foster St
Cobden Sq
Wellington
Adld Sq
HM Prison
BROMHAM ROAD
Beckett St
Hosp
St Loyes St
Pol Stn
Bus Stn
GREYFRIARS – RIVER STREET
Allhallows
Midland Road
Harpur Centre
Corn Exchange
HORNE LANE
Theatre
Rowing Club
County Hall
Bedford College of FE
CAULDWELL
Bedford St Johns
BRITANNIA ROAD
King's
Bedford Hospital
A&E
Bedfordshire Golf Club
Bromham Road
Darlow Drive
Biddenham Turn
St Gregorys Middle School
A428
Beverley Gv
Beverley Crs
Biddenham Upper School
Queen's Park
Westfield Middle School
St Josephs Lower Sch
Queens Park Lower Sch
Marlborough Lower Sch
Cutcliffe Pl
Cutcliffe Gv
Westfield Rd
All Saints Rd
Winifred Road
Hurst Grove
Preston Rd
Dunville Rd
Gratton Rd
Coventry Road
Howard Av
Marlborough Road
Westbourne Rd
Iddesleigh Road
Cromwell Road
Fairfax Rd
Ford End Road
Onsbr Cl
The Finches
St Bedes Middle Sch
ASHBURNHAM ROAD
The Av
Conduit Rd
Woburn Rd
Gibbons Rd
Rutland Rd
Alexandra Rd
Alexandra Pl
Brereton Rd
Priory St
Midland Rd
Bedford Station
PREBEND STREET
Commercial Rd
Havelock Street
MK40
Carlisle Road
Chester Road
Oldfield Road
Hawthorne Av
Allen Cl
Chestnut Av
Laburnum Av
Saunders Gdns
Works
Old Ford End Road
Ormesby Way
Wingfield Cl
Ouseland Rd
St Paul's Rd
Trinity Rd
Hill Road
Honey Hill Road
Nelson St
Raleigh St
Sikh Temple
Woodstock Rd
River Great Ouse
Marina Court
Riverside Cl
Whitbread Av
Stafford Rd
KEMPSTON ROAD
B531
Victoria Road
Edward Road
Cauldwell Walk
Cauldwell Lower Sch
Aspley Rd
Ombly Rd
Millbrook
Sandhurst Rd
Offa Road
Bunyan Rd
Muswell Rd
College Road
Eastville Rd
Odell Close
Hillgrounds Road
Gilbert Close
Mortimer Road
Loveridge Av
Viking Grove
Hartwell Drive
Ripon Cl
Wells Cl
Elm Way
Kempston Swimming Pool
St Johns Special School
Canterbury
Lichfield Cl
Westminster Gdns
Prentice Gdns
Marlborough Pk
Beatrice St
Marne St
Dallas Road
Ryswick Road
Walcourt
Malakand Road
Normandy Cl
Park Road
Stanton Rd
Slater Cl
Garden
Emmerton Rd
Vineyard
Grange School
KEMPSTON
Midland Structures Industrial Est
1 grid square represents 500 metres

Putnoe
BEDFORD
Fenlake
Bedford Park
Newnham Middle School
St John Rigby Lower School
Goldington Middle School
De Montfort University Bedford
Bedford Lawn Tennis Club
Riverside Lawn Tennis Club
Bedford Hospital (North Wing)
Bedford RUFC
Bedford School
Castle Lower School
Russell Park
Bedford Rowing Club
Dame Alice Harpur School
Bedford Athletic Stadium
Fire Station
Aspects Leisure Centre
Bowling Alley
Industrial Estate
Travel Inn
Marina
Superstore
Oasis Swimming Pool
Fenlake Road Industrial Est
Shackleton Lower Sch
Stephenson Lower School
Harrowden Middle School
Jubilee Park
GOLDINGTON ROAD
A428
A5140
LONGHOLME WAY
ROPE WALK A5140
CARDINGTON ROAD
A603
A600
LONDON ROAD
EASTCOTTS ROAD
ST JOHN'S STREET
The Embankment
River Great Ouse
13
22
31

22
Farm
Lower School
Woodcote
Queen's Drive
Mount Drive
Corniand
Barley Way
Fieldside
The Spinney
Edison Road
Caxton Road
14
A
B
C
D
507
08
Heronscroft
Meadway
The Boundary
Vicars Wk
Church Lane
The Copse
Elms Industrial Estate
Shuttleworth Rd
Goldington
Malvern Av
Purbeck Close
Portland Close
Cricket Cl
Bedford Cricket Club
Bury Wk
Ballinghall Cl
Goldington Green
Manor Road
Everard Rd
Ouse Road
Harvey Rd
Abbey Rd
PO
Perkins Rd
River Great Ouse
Innkeeper's Lodge
A428
GOLDINGTON RD
ROAD
Chapel Cl
Superstore
Marshall Ct
Grange Road
Sandy Rd
Goldington Green Lower School
Pearmain Cl
Kg Edward Rd
Alexandra Rd
Honeysuckle Way
Addington Close
Mountbatten Pl
Barker's Lane
Risborough Road
Wendover Drive
Mitre Cl
Drive
Longleat
Harpenden Cl
Bishops Road
Hatfield Crescent
Coles Cl
Kimble Drive
Aylesbury Road
Roseby Way
Avenue
Harrold Priory
Kimble Dr
Riverfield
Laycock Abby
Cartmel Priory
Bindon Abbey
Finch Pry
Industrial Estate
Brunel Road
Barker's Lane
Glastonbury Abbey
Riverfield Drive
Neath Abbey
Lindisfarne Priory
Tintern Abbey
New Cut
21
Barker's Lane
Travel Inn
Priory Country Park
Visitor Centre
A421
Meadow Lane
Stannard Way
Priory Business Park
Bedford Town FC
249
CAMBRIDGE
Fraser Road
The Barns Hotel
1
2
3
4
5
50
51
EASTCOTTS ROAD
Brampton Cl
Bamford
Alburgh Cl
Leith Rd
Arkwright Road Industrial Est
St Martins Wy
St Martins Way
St Martins Business Centre
Telford Way
Aston Rd
A5134
32
Cardington Cross
CAMBRIDGE ROAD
Bedford
1 grid square represents 500 metres

NEOTS
E
F
15
G
H
10
11
51
I
A421
River Gre
2
Willington
Lower School
Churchill Pl
Church End
Church Road
50
Balls Lane
Works
Manor Farm
3
24
Octagon
Farm
BEDFORD ROAD
Dog Farm
A603
4
A603
All Saints
Rd
249
Rye
Crs
5
Willington Road
Cople
Lower School
Burrsholt
10
11
Chapel
End
E
F
33
G
Cople
H
Cople Road

NEOTS ROAD
24
A421
A
B
16
C
D
511
12
51
1
River Great Ouse
2
Willington Lower School
Chapel Lane
Mowbray Pl
Churchill Pl
50
Russell Dr
Church Road
Station Road
Gostwick Place
Garden Centre
Barford Road
Balls Lane
3
Grange Way
Willington
Willo Farm
23
PO
SANDY
ROAD
A603
ROAD
Wood Lane
4
249
Wood Lane
5
Hill Farm
511
12
A
B
C
D
1 grid square represents 500 metres

Bedford Road
The Hill
Park Lane
Park Vw
The Avenue
Station Road
Cemetery
Old Station Ct
Chalton
The Crescent
Blunham Road
Moggerhanger Lower School
West Way
Moggerhanger
BEDFORD ROAD
A603
Dynes Place
Park Road
Park Close
St John's Road
Park Hospital
17
26
E
F
G
H
1
2
3
4
5
14
15
51
50
249

26
Brickhill Close
Lower School
River Ivel
The Hill
Wellsfield
Park Vw
Park Lane
PO
A
B
C
D
515
16
The Avenue
Station Road
Cemetery
1
2
3
4
5
Old Station Ct
South Mills
Works
The Ridgeway Business Park
The Ridgeway
25
A603
249
50
51
LONDON ROAD
A1
Dane Hill Farm
Kestrel Wy
Partridge Piece
Merlin
Wdcock Cl
Hawk Dr
The Harriers
Robin Cl
Falcon Cl
Avct Cl
Kestrel
Havelock Cl
Georgetown
Georgetown Rd
Works
Cottage Rd
Pym's Wy
Belam Way
Bunyan Rd
Waverly Av
Stirling Cl
Tallsman
Engayne
Kingsley Ct
Midland Rd
Carter St
Western Wy
Rowan Court
Oak Cl
St Neots Rd
East Road
Works
Nursery Drive
Manor Road
Western Wy
All Saints Wy
London Rd
Allhallows
West Road
South Road
Arran Cl
Banks Dr
Sandford Rl
Girtford Crs
Queen's Road
Poplar Gv
Spring Grove
Church Pth
Laburnum Rd
Laburnum Lower School
B1042
BEDFORD
The AV
Gdns
Mayfield Ct
Rivermead Gdns
Swan La
Coopers Cl
Mill Lane
Birch Grove
HIGH
Ash Cl
Elder Cl
Lime Av
Mow Cl
Grange Gdns
The Knolls
Hatch
1 grid square represents 500 metres

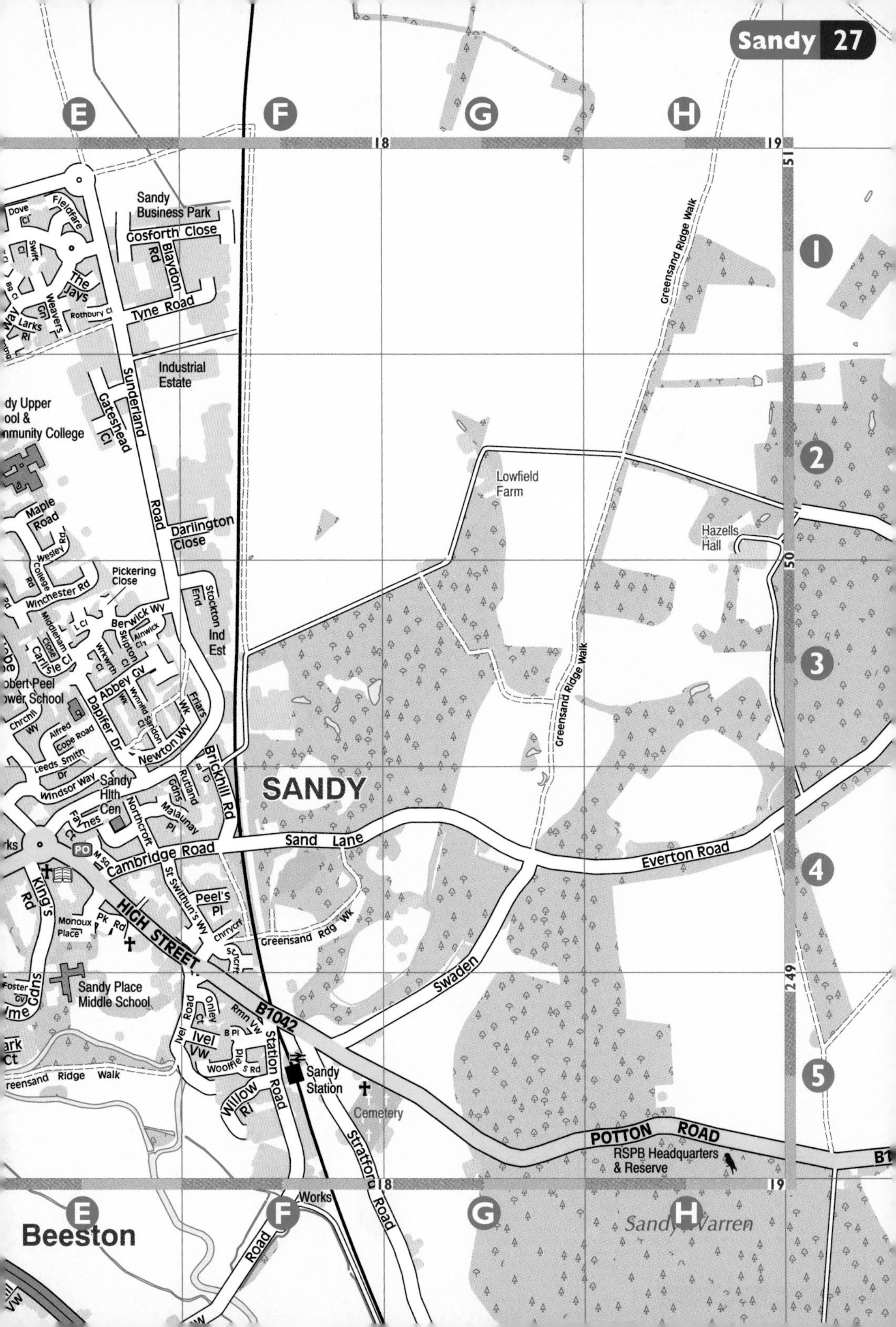
SANDY
Sandy Business Park
Gosforth Close
Blaydon Rd
Tyne Road
Rothbury Cl
Industrial Estate
Sunderland Road
Gateshead Cl
Dove Cl
Fieldfare
Swift Cl
The Jays
Weavers Grn
Larks Ri
Sandy Upper School & Community College
Maple Road
Wesley Rd
College Rd
Winchester Rd
Darlington Close
Pickering Close
Stockton End
Stockton Ind Est
Middleham Close
Carlisle Cl
Berwick Wy
Skipton Cl
Alnwick Cl
Wrkwrth Cl
Abbey Gv
Robert Peel Lower School
Chrchll Wy
Alfred Cope Road
Dapifer Dr
Wynnfld Sandon Cl
Friars Wk
Newton Wy
Brickhill Rd
Leeds Smith Dr
Windsor Way
Sandy Hlth Cen
Faynes Ct
Northcroft
Rutland Gdns
Malaunay Pl
Cambridge Road
Sand Lane
Everton Road
King's Rd
Monoux Place
Pk Rd
HIGH STREET
St Swithun's Wy
Peel's Pl
Chrrycrft
Greensand Rdg Wk
Swaden
Sandy Place Middle School
Foster Gv
B1042
Ivel Road
Onley Ct
Rmn Vw
Ivel Vw
Woolfield
Station Road
Willow Ri
Sandy Station
Cemetery
Stratford Road
Greensand Ridge Walk
POTTON ROAD
RSPB Headquarters & Reserve
Lowfield Farm
Hazells Hall
Sandy Warren
Works
Road
Beeston
E
F
G
H
I
18
19
51
50
249
2
3
4
5

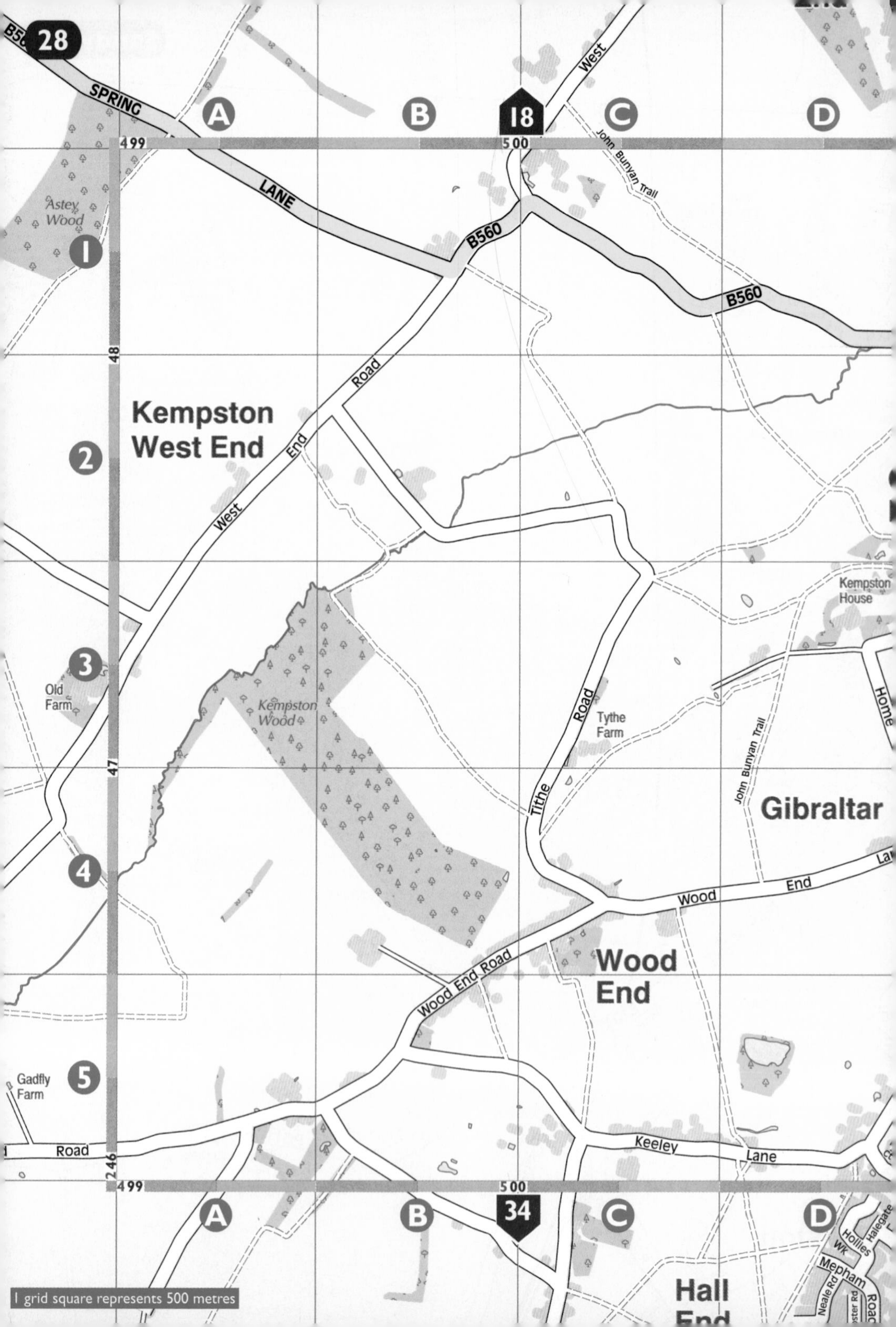

28
18
34
A
B
C
D
1
2
3
4
5
499
500
48
47
246
SPRING LANE
B560
West End Road
West
John Bunyan Trail
Astey Wood
Kempston West End
Old Farm
Kempston Wood
Tithe Road
Tythe Farm
Kempston House
Home
Gibraltar
Wood End
Wood End Road
Wood End
Gadfly Farm
Road
Keeley Lane
Hall End
Hollies Wk
Halegate
Mepham Road
Neale Rd
1 grid square represents 500 metres

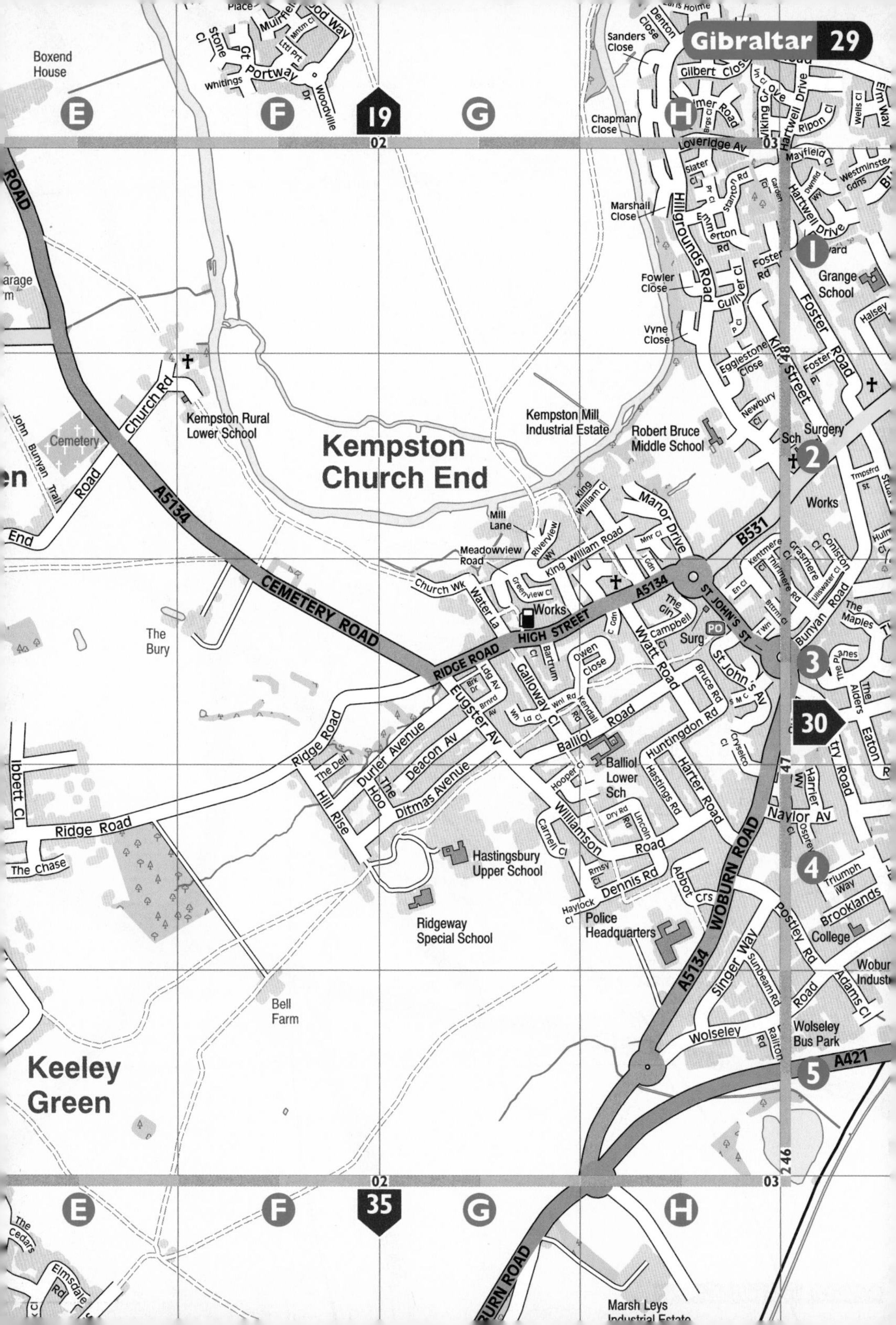
Gibraltar 29
Boxend House
Whitings
Portway
Woodville Dr
19
02
03
E
F
G
H
I
Sanders Close
Denton Close
Gilbert Close
Chapman Close
Loveridge Av
Viking Grove
Hartwell Drive
Ripon Cl
Wells Cl
Elm Way
Mayfield Cl
Westminster Gdns
Slater Cl
Stanton Rd
Marshall Close
Hillgrounds Road
Emmerton Rd
Foster Rd
Fowler Close
Gulliver Cl
Vyne Close
Grange School
Foster Road
Foster Pl
Eggleston Close
Kilpin Street
Newbury Cl
Halsey
Church Rd
Kempston Rural Lower School
Cemetery
John Bunyan Trail
Road
End
Kempston Church End
Kempston Mill Industrial Estate
Robert Bruce Middle School
Sch
Surgery
2
Works
B531
Coniston Cl
Grasmere
Kentmere
Thirlmere Rd
Ullswater Cl
Bunyan Road
The Maples
A5134
CEMETERY ROAD
Mill Lane
Riverview Wy
King William Cl
King William Road
Manor Drive
Mnr Cl
Meadowview Road
Church Wk
Water La
Greenview Cl
Works
HIGH STREET
RIDGE ROAD
ST JOHN'S ST
The Gin
Campbell Cl
Surg
PO
St John's Av
3
The Planes
The Alders
30
Eaton
The Bury
Ridge Road
The Dell
Durler Avenue
Deacon Av
Eugster Av
Galloway Cl
Bartrum
Owen Close
Wyatt Road
Bruce Rd
Kendall Rd
Balliol Road
Balliol Lower Sch
Huntingdon Rd
Cryselco Cl
Hastings Rd
Harter Road
Hooper Cl
Hill Rise
The Hoo
Ditmas Avenue
Ibbett Cl
Ridge Road
The Chase
Carnell Cl
Williamson Road
Lincoln Rd
Dry Rd
Harrier Wy
Naylor Av
Osprey Cl
4
Triumph Way
Hastingsbury Upper School
Dennis Rd
Abbot Crs
WOBURN ROAD
Brooklands College
Postley Rd
Ridgeway Special School
Haylock Cl
Police Headquarters
Singer Way
Sunbeam Rd
Adams Cl
Road
Bell Farm
Wolseley
Railton Rd
Wolseley Bus Park
A421
5
Keeley Green
246
47
35
The Cedars
Elmsdale Rd
BURN ROAD
Marsh Leys Industrial Estate

30
20
29
36
A
B
C
D
1
2
3
4
5
KEMPSTON
South End
Kempston Swimming Pool
St Johns Special School
Cauldwell Lower Sch
Midland Structures Industrial Est
Grange School
Council Building
Camestone Lower Sch
Springfield Lower School
Woburn Road Industrial Estate
Interchange Retail Park
Brooklands College
Wolseley Bus Park
Bruce School
Surgery
Works
Hillgrounds Road
Bedford Road
Ampthill Road
Elstow Road
Woburn Road
Progress Way
West End
Victoria Road
Cauldwell Walk
College Street
Spring Road
Park Road
Foster Road
Orchard Street
The Links
Chantry Road
Chantry Avenue
Eaton Road
Bunyan Road
Postley Rd
Singer Way
Wolseley Road
Harter Road
St John's St
Silverdale Street
Margetts Road
Springfield Av
Westdale Wk
Eastdale Close
Southfields Rd
Abbey Road
Offa Road
B531
A6
A421
A5134
1 grid square represents 500 metres

Fenlake
Harrowden
Shortstown
Elstow
MK42
Jubilee Park
Stephenson Lower School
Harrowden Middle School
John Bunyan Upper School
Abbey Middle School & Swimming Pool
Shortstown Lower School
Shackleton Lower Sch
Bedford Business Centre
Industrial Est
Works
Health Cen
Medbury Farm
John Bunyan Trail
A600
LONDON ROAD
A603
A5134
MILE ROAD
HARROWDEN ROAD
EASTCOTTS ROAD
B562
Old Harrowden Road
Kelvin Avenue
Brackley Road
Gloucester Road
Harewood Road
Pearcey Road
Conquest Rd
Lancaster Av
Kent Av
Broad Av
Windsor Rd
Esser Gardens
Monmouth Cl
Edinburgh Cl
Willow Rd
Dents Road
Cedar Road
Acacia
Hazelwood Road
Oak Road
Canvin Way
Barford
Faldo Rd
Clifford Road
Redwood Grove
Firbank Rd
Grosvenor St
Vulcan St
Bassie Close
Nash Rd
Mareth Road
Alamein Av
Avenue
Goodmayes Cl
Reddall Close
Bamford Road
Lovell Road
Barton Rd
Leith Rd
Harrowden Rd
Dunham Cl
Brampton Cl
Alburgh Cl
Arkwright Rd
Winchester Road
Meadowsweet Dr
Foxglove Way
Marigold Way
Wildflower Way
Lily Close
Violet Close
Harrowden Lane
Duchess Rd
Herbrand Rd
Luke Place
Berkeley Rd
Pilgrims Way
Gostwick Rd
Blundell Pl
Mowbray Road
Stapleton Rd
Corby Close
Moor Lane
Dahl Cl
Bunyans Mead
Romsey Wy
Titchfield Dr
Whitby Wy
Abbey Fields
Croxden Wy
Tewkesbury Rd
Bayham Cl
Waltham Dr
Lilleshall Dr
Melrose Drive
Dorchester Wy
Croyland Drive
Halesowen Dr
Wilstead Road
Medbury La
Pear Tree Vw
Lynn Cl
Moss La
South Av
Blenheim Rd
Lancaster Road
Lincoln Road
Halifax Rd
Whitley Rd
Canberra Rd
Stirling Road
Concorde Close
E
F
G
H
21
32
37
06
07
48
47
246
2
3
4
5

32
Ouse
The Barns Hotel
A
B
C
D
22
507
08
Fraser Road
CAMBRIDGE
Arkwright Road Industrial Est
St Martins Business Centre
Brampton Cl
Bamford
EASTCOTTS ROAD
Alburgh Cl
St Martins Wy
St Martins Way
Telford Way
A5134
Cambridge Rd
Cardington Cross
Leith Rd
Barton Rd
Road
Aston Rd
Arkwright Rd
CAMBRIDGE ROAD
Bedford Road
B562
A5134
Cambridge Road Industrial Estate
Howards House
Harrowden Rd
48
EN ROAD
Eastcotts
A600
Harrowden Lane
Cemetery
Church La
Yeomans Gate
PO
Duchess Road
Herbrand Rd
Violet Close
Way
Holm Oak Green
Church La
Cardington
Paul Waller Av
Southill Road
Old Harrowden Road
East Square
Compass Dr
North Dr
Bell's Cl
Whittley Rd
31
47
Lancaster Road
Road
Rd
Lincoln
Halifax Rd
Central Av
PO
South Dr
Greycote
Canberra Rd
Stirling Road
Concorde Close
Brancker Av
De Havilland Av
Thomson Av
Scott Av
Building Research Establishment
rtstown
er School
Shortstown
Sunderland Pl
HIGH ROAD
246
38
A600
Cotton End
1 grid square represents 500 metres

23
E
F
G
H
Cople
Lower School
Willington Road
Burrsholt
10
11
Chapel
End
Cople
Cople Road
Chapel Lane
Woodlands
Cl
Water
End
Water
End
Northill Road
Middle
Wood End
Farm
Pasture
Farm
48
47
46
2
I
2
3
4
5
39

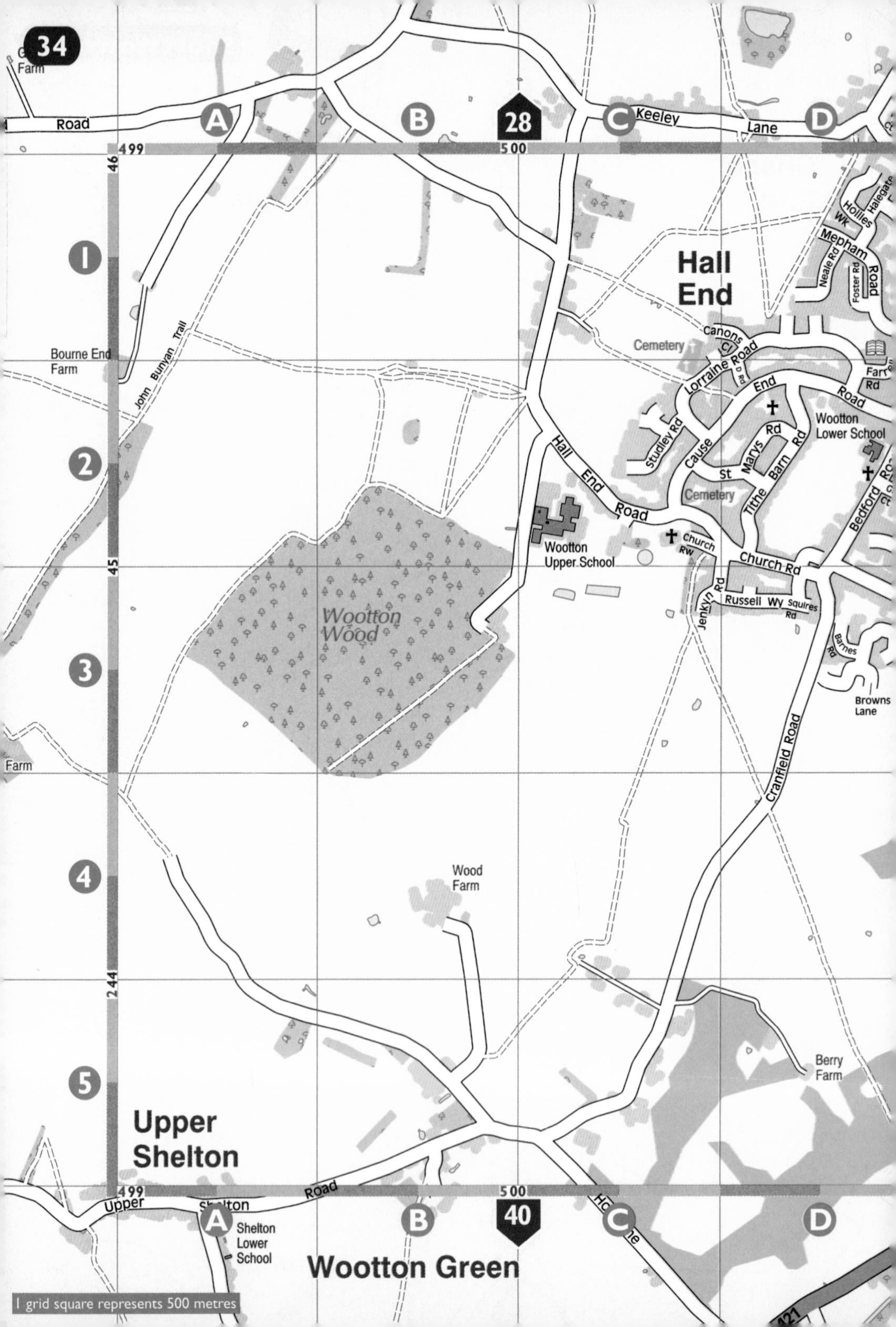
Road
Keeley Lane
28
499
500
46
45
244
Hall End
Cemetery
Canons Cl
Lorraine Road
Cause End Road
Farrell Rd
Wootton Lower School
Studley Rd
St Marys Rd
Tithe Barn Rd
Hall End Road
Wootton Upper School
Church Rw
Church Rd
Jenkyn Rd
Russell Wy
Squires Rd
Barnes Rd
Browns Lane
Bedford Road
Hollies Wk
Halegate
Mepham Road
Neale Rd
Foster Rd
Bourne End Farm
John Bunyan Trail
Wootton Wood
Farm
Cranfield Road
Wood Farm
Berry Farm
Upper Shelton
Upper Shelton Road
Shelton Lower School
Wootton Green
40
A
B
C
D
1
2
3
4
5
421
1 grid square represents 500 metres

Keeley Green
Wootton 35
Bus Park
29
E
F
G
H
02
03
46
The Cedars
Elmsdale Rd
Oak Cl
Potters Cross
Manor Rd
WOBURN ROAD
Marsh Leys Industrial Estate
I
Wootton
Elm Farm
Manor Road
2
Monoux Rd
Haycroft
Haycroft Ct
Stewart Ct
Fields Road
A421
Works
45
LC
3
Kempston Hardwick Station
Manor Road
36
Kempston Hardwick
Works
Manor
4
244
5
LC
02
03
41
E
F
G
H
Wootton Broadmead

Wolseley
Railton Rd
Wolseley Bus Park
36
A421
A6
A
B
30
C
D
503
04
46
1
AMPTHILL
Works
Works
Stanley Works
HARDWICK HILL
2
Works
45
3
Manor Road
35
Wat
Works
Manor Road
4
Wilstead Industrial Park
244
Industrial Estate
BEDFORD
5
ROAD
503
04
Lane
A
B
42
C
D
Thickthorn
Little Thickthorn Farm
Thickthorn Lane
1 grid square represents 500 metres

E
F
31
G
H
06
07
46
John Bunyan Trail
1
2
45
3
38
4
244
5
BEDFORD ROAD
Wilstead Industrial Park
Works
Dane Lane
Duck End
Duck End Lane
Works
A6
Vicarage Farm
Bedford Road
The Square
Dines Cl
Town Cl
Black Hat Close
Works
Church Rd
Luton Road
PO
Castle Cl
Cotton End Road
Chapel La
Northwood La
Brambles
Hampton Cl
Wilstead Lower School
Armstr
06
43
E
F
G
H
Home Cl
Pollards
Vicarage La
Church Farm Avenue
Wilstead
Howard

32
37
A
B
C
D
1
2
3
4
5
507
08
46
45
244
A600
Cotton End Lower School
Hermitage Gdns
Bell Lane
Cotton End
Manor Way
The Crescent
Trow Cl
Hall Way
PO
Wood Lane
Meeting Cl
Bunkers Dr
Herring's Green
Wilstead Road
Littleworth
Cotton End Road
Elms Lane
Hooked Lane
Northwood La
Ivy Lane
End Road
Brambles
Armstrong Cl
Whitworth Way
Manor Farm
John Bunyan
1 grid square represents 500 metres

Pasture Farm
E
F
33
G
H
10
11
46
1
2
Southill Road
45
The Gables
3
Exeter Wood
4
Lane
244
Warden Little Wood
5
E
F
G
H
Warden Great Wood

Upper Shelton
Berry Farm
A
B
34
C
D
499
500
Upper Shelton Road
Hoo Lane
Shelton Lower School
Wootton Green
1
A421
43
Lower Shelton Road
Chequers Close
Stratford Way
Stratford Wy
2
BEDFORD ROAD
Lower Shelton
Roberts Dr
Campin Cl
Lwr Shelton Rd
Snagge Ct
Allen Ct
Bedford Rd
Lakeview
Stewartby Lake Country Park
3
Caulcott
Beancroft Farm
Barkers Piece
42
Road
Arundel Road
Hockley Court
Parrish Close
Arundel Rd
Ingram Cl
Johnson Cl
Moreteyne Road
Bedford
4
Travelodge
Denton Dr
Chandlers
Beancroft Road
Churchill Rd
Hillson Cl
PO
Holme Cl
Scotchbrook Rd
Denton Drive
Primrose Cl
Tylecote Cl
Browns Cl
Reynes Cl
Squires Road
Moat Farm
Church Wk
The Cn
St Mary's Cl
Station Road
5
Ashcraft Close
Howes Dr
Woburn Road
Banks Close
Church End Lower School
Brk Rd
Manor Road
Manor Road
241
A
B
C
D
Marston Moretaine
1 grid square represents 500 metres

Wootton Broadmead
Broadmead Road
Stewartby
Lower School
Broadmead Business Park
Works
Broadmead Bus Park
LC
Pillinge Road
Park Crescent
Rousbury Road
Russet Cl
Churchill Close
PO
Stewartby Way
Stewartby Station
Alexander Close
The Mdw
Kitchener Place
Wavell Close
Mntgm Cl
The Crescent
Marston Vale Middle School
Road Farm
Manor Farm
E
F
G
H
1
2
3
4
5
02
03
43
42
241
35
42

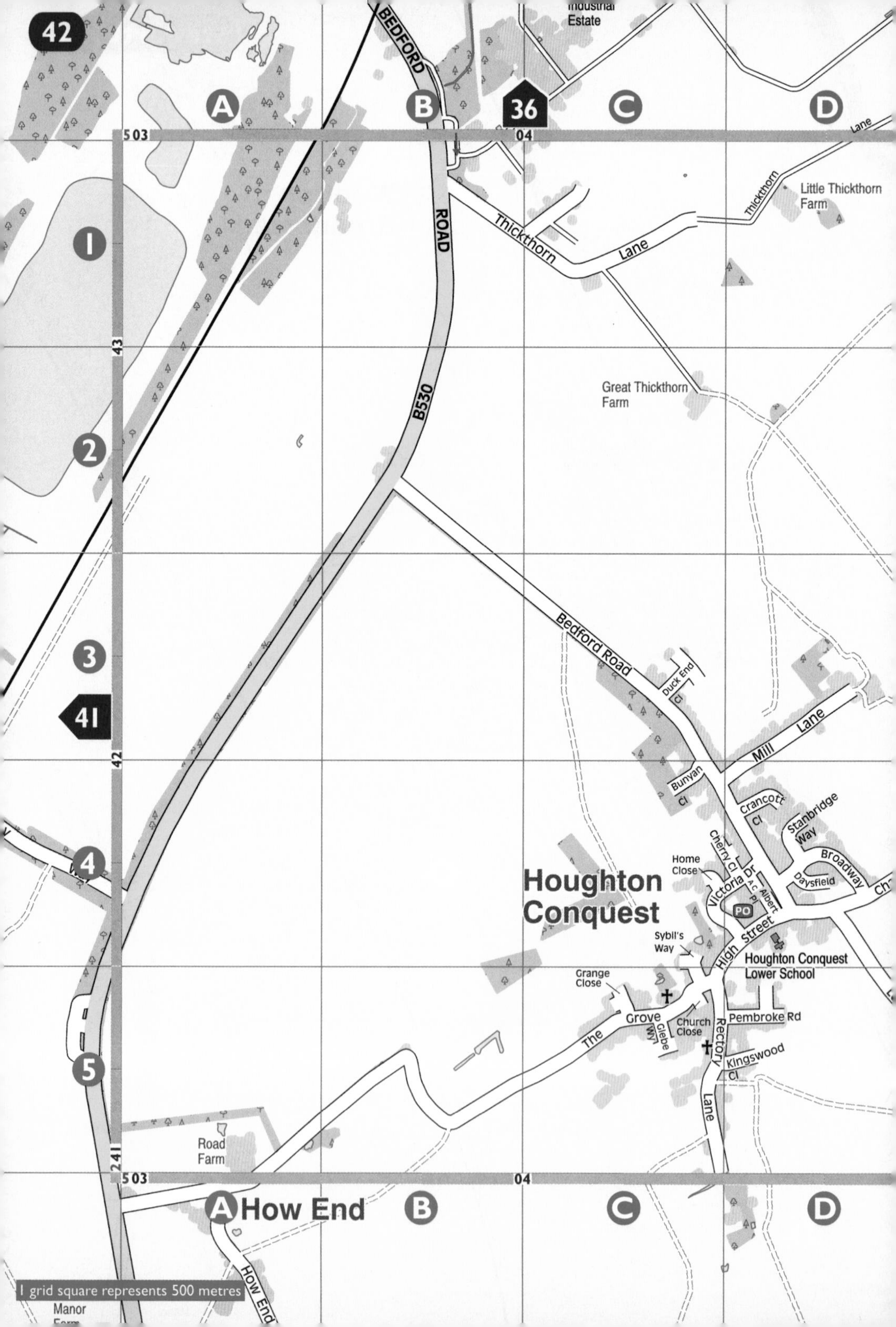
Industrial
Estate
A
B
C
D
36
503
04
BEDFORD
ROAD
B530
Thickthorn
Lane
Thickthorn
Little Thickthorn
Farm
Great Thickthorn
Farm
1
2
3
4
5
43
42
241
41
Bedford Road
Duck End
Cl
Mill
Lane
Bunyan
Cl
Crancott
Cl
Stanbridge
Way
Broadway
Daysfield
Cherry Cl
Home
Close
Victoria Dr
Albert
PO
Houghton
Conquest
High
Street
Houghton Conquest
Lower School
Sybil's
Way
Grange
Close
The
Grove
Glebe
Wy
Church
Close
Rectory
Lane
Pembroke Rd
Kingswood
Cl
Road
Farm
How End
How End
Manor
1 grid square represents 500 metres

Wilstead
Chapel End
Church Farm Avenue
Luton Road
Howard Cl
Vicarage La
Pollards Cl
Home Cl
Church Rd
Black Hat Close
The Square
Wilstead Lower School
Hampton Cl
Whitworth Way
Armstrong Cl
Brambles
Castle Cl
PO
Wilstead Wood
West Park Farm
Chapel End Road
WILSTEAD HILL
Lark Hill
Brookside Farm
Main Road
37
06
07
43
42
241
E
F
G
H
I
2
3
4
5

Bedford 2 B5
Biddenham 19 G2
Blunham 17 H5
Box End 18 D5
Brickhill 13 F4
Bridge End 19 E1
Bromham 10 C4
Cardington 32 C2
Caulcott 40 A3
Chalton 25 H2
Chapel End 33 E1
Chapel End 43 F3
Church End 8 B4
Clapham 11 H1
Clapham Green 12 B2
Cleat Hill 7 G5
Cople 33 H1
Cotton End 38 D2
Duck End 37 F4
Duck's Cross 9 H1
Eastcotts 32 A2
East End 9 H2
Elms Fm 14 C5
Elstow 31 E4
Fenlake 31 G1
Gibraltar 28 D4
Goldington 22 B1
Great Barford 17 E3
Green End 16 C3
Green End 28 D2
Hall End 34 C1
Harrowden 31 H3
Herring's Green 38 C3
Houghton Conquest 42 B4
Keeley Green 29 E5
Kempston 30 A1
Kempston Church End 29 F2
Kempston Hardwick 35 H4
Kempston West End 28 A2
Littleworth 38 C4
Lower Shelton 40 A2
Moggerhanger 25 G4
Mowsbury Park 13 H3
Oakley 4 D5
Park End 10 B1
Pavenham 4 A1
Putnoe 13 G5
Queen's Park 20 A3
Ravensden 8 B3
Renhold 15 E2
Salph End 14 B3
Sandy 27 F4
Sevick End 9 F4
Shortstown 31 H4
South End 30
South Mills 26
Stevington 10
Stewartby 41
Upper Shelton 34
Water End 33
Wilden 9
Willington 24
Wilstead 43
Wood End 7
Wood End 28
Woodside 14
Wootton 35
Wootton Broadmead 41
Wootton Green 40
Workhouse End 15

USING THE STREET INDEX

Street names are listed alphabetically. Each street name is followed by its postal town or area locality, the Postcode District, the page number, and the reference to the square in which the name is found.

Standard index entries are shown as follows:

Ballinghall Cl *BEDN* MK41 ....**22** A1

Street names and selected addresses not shown on the map due to scale restrictions are shown in the index with an asterisk:

Addison Howard Pk *KMP* * MK42 ....**30** A1

GENERAL ABBREVIATIONS

Abbreviation	Meaning
ACC	ACCESS
ALY	ALLEY
AP	APPROACH
AR	ARCADE
ASS	ASSOCIATION
AV	AVENUE
BCH	BEACH
BLDS	BUILDINGS
BND	BEND
BNK	BANK
BR	BRIDGE
BRK	BROOK
BTM	BOTTOM
BUS	BUSINESS
BVD	BOULEVARD
BY	BYPASS
CATH	CATHEDRAL
CEM	CEMETERY
CEN	CENTRE
CFT	CROFT
CH	CHURCH
CHA	CHASE
CHYD	CHURCHYARD
CIR	CIRCLE
CIRC	CIRCUS
CL	CLOSE
CLFS	CLIFFS
CMP	CAMP
CNR	CORNER
CO	COUNTY
COLL	COLLEGE
COM	COMMON
COMM	COMMISSION
CON	CONVENT
COT	COTTAGE
COTS	COTTAGES
CP	CAPE
CPS	COPSE
CR	CREEK
CREM	CREMATORIUM
CRS	CRESCENT
CSWY	CAUSEWAY
CT	COURT
CTRL	CENTRAL
CTS	COURTS
CTYD	COURTYARD
CUTT	CUTTINGS
CV	COVE
CYN	CANYON
DEPT	DEPARTMENT
DL	DALE
DM	DAM
DR	DRIVE
DRO	DROVE
DRY	DRIVEWAY
DWGS	DWELLINGS
E	EAST
EMB	EMBANKMENT
EMBY	EMBASSY
ESP	ESPLANADE
EST	ESTATE
EX	EXCHANGE
EXPY	EXPRESSWAY
EXT	EXTENSION
F/O	FLYOVER
FC	FOOTBALL CLUB
FK	FORK
FLD	FIELD
FLDS	FIELDS
FLS	FALLS
FLS	FLATS
FM	FARM
FT	FORT
FWY	FREEWAY
FY	FERRY
GA	GATE
GAL	GALLERY
GDN	GARDEN
GDNS	GARDENS
GLD	GLADE
GLN	GLEN
GN	GREEN
GND	GROUND
GRA	GRANGE
GRG	GARAGE
GT	GREAT
GTWY	GATEWAY
GV	GROVE
HGR	HIGHER
HL	HILL
HLS	HILLS
HO	HOUSE
HOL	HOLLOW
HOSP	HOSPITAL
HRB	HARBOUR
HTH	HEATH
HTS	HEIGHTS
HVN	HAVEN
HWY	HIGHWAY
IMP	IMPERIAL
IN	INLET
IND EST	INDUSTRIAL ESTATE
INF	INFIRMARY
INFO	INFORMATION
INT	INTERCHANGE
IS	ISLAND
JCT	JUNCTION
JTY	JETTY
KG	KING
KNL	KNOLL
L	LAKE
LA	LANE
LDG	LODGE
LGT	LIGHT
LK	LOCK
LKS	LAKES
LNDG	LANDING
LTL	LITTLE
LWR	LOWER
MAG	MAGISTRATE
MAN	MANSIONS
MD	MEAD
MDW	MEADOWS
MEM	MEMORIAL
MKT	MARKET
MKTS	MARKETS
ML	MALL
ML	MILL
MNR	MANOR
MS	MEWS
MSN	MISSION
MT	MOUNT
MTN	MOUNTAIN
MTS	MOUNTAINS
MUS	MUSEUM
MWY	MOTORWAY
N	NORTH
NE	NORTH EAST
NW	NORTH WEST
O/P	OVERPASS
OFF	OFFICE
ORCH	ORCHARD
OV	OVAL
PAL	PALACE
PAS	PASSAGE
PAV	PAVILION
PDE	PARADE
PH	PUBLIC HOUSE
PK	PARK
PKWY	PARKWAY
PL	PLACE
PLN	PLAIN
PLNS	PLAINS
PLZ	PLAZA
POL	POLICE STATION
PR	PRINCE
PREC	PRECINCT
PREP	PREPARATORY
PRIM	PRIMARY
PROM	PROMENADE
PRS	PRINCESS
PRT	PORT
PT	POINT
PTH	PATH
PZ	PIAZZA
QD	QUADRANT
QU	QUEEN
QY	QUAY
R	RIVER
RBT	ROUNDABOUT
RD	ROAD
RDG	RIDGE
REP	REPUBLIC
RES	RESERVOIR
RFC	RUGBY FOOTBALL CLUB
RI	RISE
RP	RAMP
RW	ROW
S	SOUTH
SCH	SCHOOL
SE	SOUTH EAST
SER	SERVICE AREA
SH	SHORE
SHOP	SHOPPING
SKWY	SKYWAY
SMT	SUMMIT
SOC	SOCIETY
SP	SPUR
SPR	SPRING
SQ	SQUARE
ST	STREET
STN	STATION
STR	STREAM
STRD	STRAND
SW	SOUTH WEST
TDG	TRADING
TER	TERRACE
THWY	THROUGHWAY
TNL	TUNNEL
TOLL	TOLLWAY
TPK	TURNPIKE
TR	TRACK
TRL	TRAIL
TWR	TOWER
U/P	UNDERPASS
UNI	UNIVERSITY
UPR	UPPER
V	VALE
VA	VALLEY
VIAD	VIADUCT
VIL	VILLA
VIS	VISTA
VLG	VILLAGE
VLS	VILLAS
VW	VIEW
W	WEST
WD	WOOD
WHF	WHARF
WK	WALK
WKS	WALKS
WLS	WELLS
WY	WAY
YD	YARD
YHA	YOUTH HOSTEL

POSTCODE TOWNS AND AREA ABBREVIATIONS

Abbreviation	Meaning
AMP/FLIT/BLC	Ampthill/Flitwick/Barton-le-Clay
BED	Bedford
BEDN	Bedford north
BGSW	Biggleswade
KMP	Kempston
RBEDNE	Rural Bedford north & east
RBEDW	Rural Bedford west
SDY/GAM/POT	Sandy/Gamlingay/Potton

A

ıbey Cl AMP/FLIT/B MK45 ... 30 D3
BEDN MK41 ... 14 B1
bey Flds AMP/FLIT/B MK45 ... 30 D3
.bey Gv SDY/GAM/PO SG19 ... 27 E3
ıbey Rd BEDN MK41 ... 22 A1
bot Crs KMP MK42 ... 29 H4
acia Rd KMP MK42 ... 31 F1
lams Cl KMP MK42 ... 30 A5
ldington Cl BEDN MK41 ... 22 A2
ldingtons Rd RBEDNE MK44 ... 17 E3
ldison Cl KMP MK42 ... 30 B2
ldison Howard Pk
KMP * MK42 ... 30 A1
lelaide Sq BED MK40 ... 2 C2
ımein Av KMP MK42 ... 21 G5
bany Rd BED MK40 ... 3 F3
bert Pl AMP/FLIT/B MK45 ... 42 D4
bert St BED MK40 ... 2 D1
burgh Cl KMP MK42 ... 31 H1
denham Cl BEDN MK41 ... 22 B3
dens Md BEDN MK41 ... 14 A4
e Alders KMP MK42 ... 30 A3
exander Cl RBEDW MK43 ... 41 G3
exandra Pl BED MK40 ... 2 B3
exandra Rd BED MK40 ... 2 B3
fred Cope Rd
SDY/GAM/PO SG19 ... 27 E3
en Cl BED MK40 ... 20 B3
en Ct RBEDW MK43 ... 40 C3
hallows BED MK40 ... 2 D3
SDY/GAM/PO SG19 ... 26 D3
Saints Rd BED MK40 ... 20 B3
RBEDNE MK44 ... 23 G4
Saints Wy
SDY/GAM/PO SG19 ... 26 D3
ner's Cl AMP/FLIT/B MK45 ... 42 D4
e Almonds KMP MK42 ... 30 C3
nwick Cl SDY/GAM/PO SG19 ... 27 E3
thorpe St KMP MK42 ... 2 D7
nberley Gdns BED MK40 ... 21 F1
npthill Rd AMP/FLIT/B MK45 ... 30 C3
AMP/FLIT/B MK45 ... 36 B1
npthill St KMP MK42 ... 2 E6
e Arcade BED MK40 ... 2 D3
gyll St BED MK40 ... 20 D1
kwright Rd KMP MK42 ... 32 A1
mstrong Cl AMP/FLIT/B MK45 ... 43 H1
mstrong Dr KMP MK42 ... 21 E5
ran Cl SDY/GAM/PO SG19 ... 26 D3
row Leys BEDN MK41 ... 13 H4
un Cl BEDN MK41 ... 13 F3
undel Dr BEDN MK41 ... 14 A4
undel Rd RBEDW MK43 ... 40 B4
gard Dr BEDN MK41 ... 14 D4
hburnham Rd BED MK40 ... 2 A2
h Cl SDY/GAM/PO SG19 ... 26 D5
hcraft Cl RBEDW MK43 ... 40 A5
hdale Av KMP MK42 ... 30 B2
hridge Dr BEDN MK41 ... 14 C4
h Wk KMP MK42 ... 30 C3
spen Av BEDN MK41 ... 13 G4
spley Rd KMP MK42 ... 20 D5
ston Rd KMP MK42 ... 32 A1
therstone Abbey BEDN MK41 ... 22 B3
ustin Canons KMP * MK42 ... 20 C5
e Avenue BED MK40 ... 2 B3
RBEDNE MK44 ... 25 H1
SDY/GAM/PO SG19 ... 26 D5
ocet Cl SDY/GAM/PO SG19 ... 26 D2
on Dr BEDN MK41 ... 13 F3
lesbury Rd BEDN MK41 ... 21 H3

B

alinghall Cl BEDN MK41 ... 22 A1
alliol Rd KMP MK42 ... 29 G3
alls La RBEDNE MK44 ... 23 H3
almoral Av BED MK40 ... 21 F1
almoral Cl SDY/GAM/PO SG19 ... 26 D2
alsall St East BED MK40 ... 2 D2
alsall St West BED MK40 ... 2 D2
amburgh Dr BEDN MK41 ... 14 A4
amford Rd KMP MK42 ... 31 H1
anks Cl RBEDW MK43 ... 40 A5
anks Dr SDY/GAM/PO SG19 ... 26 D4
arford Av KMP MK42 ... 21 F5
arford Rd RBEDNE MK44 ... 9 H4
RBEDNE MK44 ... 24 D2
arker's La BEDN MK41 ... 21 H4
arkers Piece RBEDW MK43 ... 40 B3
arley Wy BEDN MK41 ... 14 A5
arnard Av KMP MK42 ... 29 G3
Barnes Rd RBEDW MK43 ... 34 D3
Barnhill BEDN MK41 ... 22 A1
Barnstaple Rd BED MK40 ... 21 G1
Barton Rd KMP MK42 ... 31 H1
Bartrum Cl KMP MK42 ... 29 G3
Bassie Cl KMP MK42 ... 2 E7
Batcheldor Gdns RBEDW MK43 ... 18 C2
Battison St BED MK40 ... 2 C4
Battle Abbey BEDN MK41 ... 22 B2
The Baulk BEDN MK41 ... 6 B4
Bayham Cl KMP MK42 ... 31 F3
Beaconsfield St BEDN MK41 ... 20 D1
Beancroft Rd RBEDW MK43 ... 40 A4
Beatrice St KMP MK42 ... 20 C5
Beauchamp Ct BED MK40 ... 2 B2
Beauchamp Rd RBEDW MK43 ... 35 E3
Beaufort Wy BEDN MK41 ... 13 E2
Becher Cl BEDN MK41 ... 15 G3
Beckett St BED MK40 ... 2 C3
Bedesman La KMP MK42 ... 2 E5
Bedford Rd AMP/FLIT/B MK45 ... 37 E2
AMP/FLIT/B MK45 ... 42 C3
BEDN MK41 ... 12 A3
KMP MK42 ... 30 A2
RBEDNE MK44 ... 5 G2
RBEDNE MK44 ... 7 G5
RBEDNE MK44 ... 16 C4
RBEDNE MK44 ... 32 C1
RBEDW MK43 ... 18 A2
RBEDW MK43 ... 34 D2
RBEDW MK43 ... 40 B4
SDY/GAM/PO SG19 ... 26 D4
Beechdale Rd KMP MK42 ... 31 E1
Beech Wk KMP MK42 ... 30 B3
Belam Wy SDY/GAM/PO SG19 ... 26 D2
Belfry Cl KMP MK42 ... 30 D2
Bell La AMP/FLIT/B MK45 ... 38 D2
Bell's Cl KMP MK42 ... 32 A3
Bents Cl BEDN MK41 ... 11 H1
Bereford Cl RBEDNE MK44 ... 16 D3
Beresford Rd BED MK40 ... 3 K4
Berkeley Rd KMP MK42 ... 31 E2
Berry Dr RBEDW MK43 ... 18 C1
Berwick Wy SDY/GAM/PO SG19 ... 27 E3
Beverley Crs BED MK40 ... 20 B2
Beverley Gv BED MK40 ... 20 A2
Bevery Cl RBEDW MK43 ... 5 E5
Bewcastle Cl BEDN MK41 ... 14 A3
Biddenham Turn BED MK40 ... 19 H2
Bindon Abbey BEDN MK41 ... 22 A3
Birchdale Av KMP MK42 ... 30 B2
Birchfield Rd RBEDNE MK44 ... 16 C1
Birch Gv SDY/GAM/PO SG19 ... 26 D5
Birkdale Rd BEDN MK41 ... 13 G3
Bishops Rd BEDN MK41 ... 22 B2
Bishopstone Ct BED * MK40 ... 2 A3
Blackburn Cl KMP MK42 ... 32 B4
Black Hat Cl AMP/FLIT/B MK45 ... 37 G5
Blaydon Rd SDY/GAM/PO SG19 ... 27 E1
Blenheim Rd KMP MK42 ... 31 H3
Blundell Pl KMP MK42 ... 31 E2
Blunham Rd RBEDNE MK44 ... 25 G4
Boswell Ct BED MK40 ... 2 C1
Boswell Pl BED MK40 ... 2 C1
The Boulevards BED * MK40 ... 2 D4
The Boundary BEDN MK41 ... 22 A1
Bourneside BEDN MK41 ... 13 F2
Bower St BED MK40 ... 3 H2
Bowhill BEDN MK41 ... 13 H5
Box End Rd RBEDW MK43 ... 18 D2
Boxgrove Priory BEDN MK41 ... 22 B2
Boyde Gdns BED MK40 ... 20 A4
Brace St BED MK40 ... 2 C3
Bracken Pl BEDN MK41 ... 22 B2
Brackley Rd KMP MK42 ... 31 E1
Bradgate Rd BED MK40 ... 3 H1
Braeside BEDN MK41 ... 13 H4
Brambles AMP/FLIT/B MK45 ... 37 H5
Brambling Cl SDY/GAM/PO SG19 ... 27 E1
Brampton Cl KMP MK42 ... 31 H1
Brancaster Cl KMP MK42 ... 31 H2
Brancker Av KMP MK42 ... 32 A4
Brandreth Pl SDY/GAM/PO SG19 ... 27 F5
Brecon Wy BEDN MK41 ... 13 G3
Brendon Av BEDN MK41 ... 21 G1
Brereton Rd BED MK40 ... 2 C3
Brett Dr RBEDW MK43 ... 18 D2
The Briars KMP MK42 ... 30 B3
Brickfield Rd BEDN MK41 ... 14 B2
Brickhill Cl SDY/GAM/PO SG19 ... 27 F4
Brickhill Dr BEDN MK41 ... 12 C5
Brickhill Rd SDY/GAM/PO SG19 ... 27 F3
Bridge Rd KMP MK42 ... 21 E5
Bridle Dr BEDN MK41 ... 11 G1
Brindley Cl SDY/GAM/PO SG19 ... 26 D2
Britannia Rd KMP MK42 ... 2 C6
Brixham Cl BED MK40 ... 21 G1
Broad Av KMP MK42 ... 31 F1
Broadhurst Abbey BEDN MK41 ... 22 A3
Broadmead Rd RBEDW MK43 ... 41 G2
Broad Reach BED * MK40 ... 3 F4
The Broadway BED MK40 ... 2 D2
Broadway AMP/FLIT/B MK45 ... 42 D4
Brockwell RBEDW MK43 ... 5 E5
Bromham Rd BED MK40 ... 2 B2
Brook Dr KMP MK42 ... 29 G3
Brookfield Rd BEDN MK41 ... 21 H1
Brookfields RBEDW MK43 ... 4 A1
Brooklands KMP MK42 ... 30 A4
Brook La BEDN MK41 ... 14 B2
RBEDNE MK44 ... 16 D2
Brook Rd RBEDW MK43 ... 40 A5
Brookside BEDN MK41 ... 14 B1
RBEDNE MK44 ... 17 E3
Brook St KMP MK42 ... 31 F1
Brook Wy RBEDW MK43 ... 18 C1
Browns Cl RBEDW MK43 ... 40 B5
Browns La RBEDW MK43 ... 34 D3
Bruce Rd KMP MK42 ... 29 H3
Brunel Rd BEDN MK41 ... 21 H3
Bryony Cl BEDN MK41 ... 22 B2
Buckfast Av BEDN MK41 ... 13 H3
Bucks Cl RBEDW MK43 ... 18 D1
Bunkers Dr AMP/FLIT/B MK45 ... 38 D2
The Buntings BEDN MK41 ... 13 F4
SDY/GAM/PO SG19 ... 27 E1
Bunyan Cl AMP/FLIT/B MK45 ... 42 C4
Bunyan Rd KMP MK42 ... 30 A3
KMP MK42 ... 30 D1
SDY/GAM/PO SG19 ... 26 D2
Bunyans Md KMP * MK42 ... 30 D2
Bure Cl BEDN MK41 ... 13 E2
Burgess Cl KMP MK42 ... 19 H5
Burleigh Pl RBEDW MK43 ... 5 E5
Burnaby Rd BED MK40 ... 2 E1
Burridge Cl RBEDW MK43 ... 40 B4
Burridge's Cl RBEDW MK43 ... 10 A1
Burrsholt RBEDNE MK44 ... 33 G1
Bury Wk BEDN MK41 ... 22 B1
Bushmead Av BED MK40 ... 3 G2
Butler St RBEDNE MK44 ... 7 G4
Butler Wy KMP MK42 ... 30 A1
Buttercup Cl KMP MK42 ... 31 G2
Buttermere Cl KMP MK42 ... 29 H3
Byron Crs BED MK40 ... 20 B1

C

Caister Rd BEDN MK41 ... 14 A4
Calder Ri BEDN MK41 ... 13 F2
Cambrian Wy BEDN MK41 ... 13 G5
Cambridge Rd KMP MK42 ... 32 B1
RBEDNE MK44 ... 22 D5
SDY/GAM/PO SG19 ... 27 E4
Campbell Cl KMP MK42 ... 29 H3
Campbell Rd BED MK40 ... 3 H1
Campin Cl RBEDW MK43 ... 40 C3
Canberra Rd KMP MK42 ... 31 H4
Cannock Cha BEDN MK41 ... 14 C4
Canons Cl RBEDW MK43 ... 34 C1
Canterbury Cl KMP MK42 ... 20 A5
Canvin Wy KMP MK42 ... 31 G1
Cardington Rd KMP MK42 ... 3 F5
Carlisle Cl SDY/GAM/PO SG19 ... 27 E3
Carlisle Rd BED MK40 ... 20 A4
Carnell Cl KMP MK42 ... 29 G4
Carnoustie Dr BED MK40 ... 19 F4
Carriage Dr BEDN MK41 ... 12 B2
Carrick Rd BEDN MK41 ... 14 B4
Carroll Dr KMP MK42 ... 31 E2
Carron Rd BEDN MK41 ... 13 E1
Carter Cl KMP MK42 ... 21 G5
Carter St SDY/GAM/PO SG19 ... 26 D3
Cartmel Priory BEDN MK41 ... 22 A3
Castle Cl AMP/FLIT/B MK45 ... 37 H5
Castle La BED MK40 ... 2 E4
Castle Rd BED MK40 ... 2 E3
Cater St KMP MK42 ... 30 A2
Cauldwell Pl KMP MK42 ... 2 D6
Cauldwell St KMP MK42 ... 2 C6
Cauldwell Wk KMP MK42 ... 20 C5
Cause End Rd RBEDW MK43 ... 34 C2
Cavendish St BED MK40 ... 2 D1
Cave's La BED MK40 ... 3 J1
Cawdor Cl BEDN MK41 ... 14 B4
Caxton Pk BEDN * MK41 ... 14 C5
Caxton Rd BEDN MK41 ... 22 C1
Cedar Cl RBEDW * MK43 ... 18 C2
Cedar Gdns SDY/GAM/PO SG19 ... 26 D4
Cedar Rd KMP MK42 ... 31 F1
The Cedars RBEDW MK43 ... 35 E1
Cemetery Rd RBEDW MK43 ... 29 F3
Central Av KMP MK42 ... 32 A4
Chagford Cl BED MK40 ... 3 K1
Chandlers Cl RBEDW MK43 ... 40 A4
Chandos St BED MK40 ... 2 C1
Chantry Av KMP MK42 ... 30 A4
Chantry Rd KMP MK42 ... 30 A3
Chapel Cl BEDN MK41 ... 22 B1
RBEDNE MK44 ... 16 D3
Chapel End Rd
AMP/FLIT/B MK45 ... 42 D4
Chapel Fld RBEDNE MK44 ... 16 C3
Chapel La AMP/FLIT/B MK45 ... 37 H5
RBEDNE MK44 ... 24 A2
RBEDNE MK44 ... 33 E1
Chapel Pound RBEDW MK43 ... 5 E5
Chapman Cl BED MK40 ... 19 H5
Charnwood Av BEDN MK41 ... 14 B4
The Chase RBEDW MK43 ... 29 E4
Chaucer Rd BED MK40 ... 20 B1
Chelmer Cl BEDN MK41 ... 13 F1
Cheltenham Cl BEDN MK41 ... 14 B5
Chequers Cl RBEDW MK43 ... 40 B2
Chequers Hl RBEDNE MK44 ... 9 G1
Cherry Cl AMP/FLIT/B MK45 ... 42 C4
Cherrycroft SDY/GAM/PO SG19 ... 27 F4
Cherry Wk KMP MK42 ... 30 B2
Cherwell Rd BEDN MK41 ... 13 E3
Chessington Cl BEDN MK41 ... 22 B3
Chester Rd BED MK40 ... 20 A3
Chestnut Av BED MK40 ... 20 B3
RBEDW MK43 ... 10 B5
Chestnut Gdns KMP * MK42 ... 30 A3
Chethams KMP MK42 ... 3 F5
Cheviot Cl BEDN MK41 ... 13 G5
Chiltern Av BEDN MK41 ... 13 G5
Chinnor Cl BEDN MK41 ... 22 B2
Christie Rd KMP MK42 ... 3 G7
Chudleigh Cl BED MK40 ... 21 G1
Church Ar BED MK40 ... 2 D3
Church Cl AMP/FLIT/B MK45 ... 42 C5
BEDN * MK41 ... 14 D2
Church End AMP/FLIT/B MK45 ... 30 D3
BED MK40 ... 19 F3
BEDN MK41 ... 14 D2
RBEDNE MK44 ... 8 B5
RBEDNE MK44 ... 23 H2
Church Farm Av
AMP/FLIT/B MK45 ... 43 G1
Churchgate RBEDNE MK44 ... 17 E4
Church Gn RBEDNE MK44 ... 5 F1
Churchill Cl RBEDW MK43 ... 41 F3
Churchill Pl RBEDNE MK44 ... 23 H2
Churchill Rd RBEDW MK43 ... 40 A4
Churchill Wy SDY/GAM/PO SG19 ... 27 E3
Church La BEDN MK41 ... 14 B4
RBEDNE MK44 ... 32 D2
RBEDW MK43 ... 4 A1
RBEDW MK43 ... 10 D2
Church Pth SDY/GAM/PO SG19 ... 26 D4
Church Rd AMP/FLIT/B MK45 ... 37 G5
RBEDNE MK44 ... 23 H3
RBEDW MK43 ... 10 A1
RBEDW MK43 ... 29 E2
RBEDW MK43 ... 34 D2
Church Rw RBEDW MK43 ... 34 C2
Church St BED MK40 ... 2 C4
Church Vw BEDN MK41 ... 12 B2
Churchville Rd KMP MK42 ... 30 D1
Church Wk KMP MK42 ... 29 G3
RBEDW MK43 ... 40 B5
Churnet Cl BEDN MK41 ... 13 E1
Clapham Rd BED MK40 ... 20 B1
BEDN MK41 ... 12 B4
Clarendon St BEDN MK41 ... 20 C1
Clare Rd BEDN MK41 ... 14 A3
Cleat Hl BEDN MK41 ... 13 G2
Cleeve Abbey BEDN MK41 ... 22 B3
Cleveland St KMP MK42 ... 30 A2
Clipstone Cl BEDN MK41 ... 14 B5
The Cloisters BEDN MK41 ... 22 B2
The Close BEDN MK41 ... 12 A3
RBEDNE MK44 ... 17 E3
Close Rd RBEDW MK43 ... 4 C2
Clovelly Wy BED MK40 ... 21 G1
Clover Av BEDN MK41 ... 22 B3
Clyde Crs BEDN MK41 ... 13 F3
Cobden Sq BED MK40 ... 2 D1
Cody Rd BEDN MK41 ... 11 H2
Colchester Wy BEDN MK41 ... 14 A3
Coles Cl BEDN MK41 ... 22 A2
Colesden Rd RBEDNE MK44 ... 9 G2
College Rd KMP MK42 ... 30 D1
SDY/GAM/PO SG19 ... 27 E3
College St KMP MK42 ... 30 C2
Collie Rd KMP MK42 ... 3 J7
Collins Pl KMP MK42 ... 31 H1
Columbine Cl BEDN MK41 ... 14 C4
Commercial Rd BED MK40 ... 2 C4
Compass Dr KMP MK42 ... 32 A3
Concorde Cl KMP MK42 ... 32 A4

Conduit Rd BED MK40 2 B2
Coniston Cl KMP MK42 30 A2
Connaught Wy BEDN MK41 13 F2
Conquest Rd KMP MK42 31 E1
Constable Hl BEDN MK41 20 C1
Conway Crs BEDN MK41 13 E3
Coombs Cl KMP MK42 3 G7
Coopers Cl RBEDNE MK44 16 C3
SDY/GAM/PO SG19 26 D5
Cople Rd RBEDNE MK44 33 F1
The Copse BEDN MK41 22 B1
Copthorne Cl RBEDW MK43 5 E5
Corby Cl KMP MK42 31 F2
Corfe Rd BEDN MK41 14 A4
Cornland BEDN MK41 14 A5
Cornwallis Cl RBEDW MK43 10 C5
Cornwall Rd BED MK40 21 F1
Cosmic Av KMP MK42 30 C2
Costin St BED MK40 2 C4
Cotman Cl BEDN MK41 12 C5
Cotswold Cl BEDN MK41 21 H1
Cottage Rd SDY/GAM/PO SG19 26 D2
Cotton End Rd
AMP/FLIT/B MK45 37 H5
Cottril Wy KMP MK42 21 G5
Countess Gdns KMP MK42 29 H3
Coventry Rd BED MK40 20 B3
Cowper Rd BED MK40 20 B1
Cox's Cl BED MK40 20 B4
Cranborne Cl BEDN MK41 14 B4
Crancott Cl AMP/FLIT/B MK45 42 D4
Cranfield Rd RBEDW MK43 34 D4
Crediton Cl BED MK40 21 G1
The Crescent AMP/FLIT/B MK45 38 D2
BED MK40 2 C2
KMP MK42 32 A3
RBEDNE MK44 25 G3
RBEDW MK43 41 G4
Cricket Cl BEDN MK41 22 A1
The Croft BEDN MK41 22 A1
Crofton Cl BEDN MK41 13 F4
Cromwell Rd BED MK40 20 B4
Crossroads AMP/FLIT/B * MK45 37 G5
Cross St BED MK40 2 D2
Crown Pl KMP MK42 2 D6
Croxden Wy KMP MK42 31 E3
Croyland Dr KMP MK42 31 F3
Cryselco Cl KMP MK42 29 H3
Curlew Crs BEDN MK41 12 D4
Cutcliffe Gdns BED MK40 20 B3
Cutcliffe Gv BED MK40 20 B3
Cutcliffe Pl BED MK40 20 B3
Cut Throat La BED MK40 20 B1
Cynthia Ct RBEDW MK43 35 E3

D

Dahl Cl KMP MK42 31 E2
Dale Cl BEDN MK41 14 A5
Dallas Rd KMP MK42 20 C5
Dame Alice St BED MK40 2 D2
Dane La AMP/FLIT/B MK45 37 E4
Dane St BED MK40 2 D3
Dapifer Dr SDY/GAM/PO SG19 27 E3
Darlington Cl
SDY/GAM/PO SG19 27 E2
Darlow Dr BED MK40 19 H2
Dart Rd BEDN MK41 13 E3
Darwin Rd KMP MK42 31 E1
Davis Cl KMP * MK42 30 D1
Dawlish Dr BED MK40 3 K1
Daysfield AMP/FLIT/B MK45 42 D4
Day's La BED MK40 19 G2
Deacon Av KMP MK42 29 G4
Deacon Ms RBEDW MK43 40 A4
Dean St BED MK40 21 H2
Deep Spinney BED MK40 19 G2
Deeside BEDN MK41 13 F3
De Havilland Av KMP MK42 32 A4
Delamare Cl SDY/GAM/PO SG19 26 D2
The Dell KMP MK42 29 F4
Denbigh Cl RBEDW MK43 40 B4
Denmark St BED MK40 3 J2
Dennis Rd KMP MK42 29 H4
Denton Cl KMP MK42 19 H5
Denton Dr RBEDW MK43 40 A5
Dents Rd KMP MK42 21 F5
De Parys Av BED MK40 20 D1
Derby Pl BED MK40 2 D1
Derwent Pl KMP MK42 20 D5
Devizes Av BEDN MK41 14 A3
Dewlands RBEDW MK43 10 D1
Dimmock Rd RBEDW MK43 34 D2
Dines Cl AMP/FLIT/B MK45 37 G5
Ditmas Av KMP MK42 29 G4
Donnelly Dr BEDN MK41 22 A2
Dorchester Wy KMP MK42 31 E3
Dorsey Dr KMP MK42 30 D1
Dothans Cl RBEDNE MK44 16 C3
Douglas Rd BEDN MK41 13 F2
Dove Cl SDY/GAM/PO SG19 27 E1
Dovehouse Cl RBEDW MK43 18 D1
Dover Crs BEDN MK41 14 A3
Dove Rd BEDN MK41 13 F4
Downfield Wy KMP MK42 30 A1
Downside BEDN MK41 14 A5
Drayton Rd KMP MK42 29 H4
The Drive RBEDW * MK43 10 D1
Duchess Rd KMP MK42 31 H2
Duck End Cl AMP/FLIT/B MK45 42 C3
Duck End La AMP/FLIT/B MK45 37 G4
BED MK40 19 F2
Duckmill Crs KMP * MK42 2 E5
KMP * MK42 3 G5
Duck Mill La KMP MK42 2 E5
Dudley Cl KMP MK42 30 A3
Dudley St BED MK40 3 J2
Duke Dr BEDN MK41 11 H1
Duke St BED MK40 2 E3
Duncombe St KMP MK42 30 A2
Dunham Cl KMP MK42 31 H1
Dunkirk Cl KMP MK42 30 B1
Dunster Gdns BEDN MK41 14 B3
Dunvegan Wy BEDN MK41 13 H3
Dunville Rd BED MK40 20 B3
Durler Av KMP MK42 29 F4
Dynes Pl RBEDNE MK44 25 G4
Dynevor Cl RBEDW MK43 18 C1
Dynevor Rd BED MK40 2 A2

E

Eagle Gdns BEDN MK41 12 D5
Earls Holme KMP MK42 19 H5
Easby Abbey BEDN MK41 22 B3
Eastcotts Rd KMP MK42 21 H5
Eastdale Cl KMP MK42 30 C2
East End La RBEDNE MK44 9 H2
East Rd SDY/GAM/PO SG19 26 D3
East Sq KMP MK42 32 A3
Eastville Rd KMP MK42 30 D1
Eaton Rd KMP MK42 30 A3
Ebble Md BEDN MK41 13 F2
Edinburgh Cl KMP MK42 31 F1
Edison Rd BEDN MK41 14 C5
Edward Rd KMP MK42 2 B7
Egglestone Cl KMP MK42 29 H2
Elder Cl SDY/GAM/PO SG19 26 D5
Elger Cl BED MK40 19 H2
Ellington Rd KMP MK42 30 D1
Elliot Crs BEDN MK41 14 B5
Ellis Rd BEDN MK41 13 F5
Elm Cl BEDN MK41 13 G4
The Elms KMP MK42 30 A3
Elmsdale Rd RBEDW MK43 35 E1
Elms La AMP/FLIT/B MK45 38 B4
Elmtree Rd SDY/GAM/PO SG19 26 D3
Elm Wy KMP MK42 20 A5
Elstow Rd KMP MK42 30 A3
KMP MK42 31 E2
The Embankment KMP MK42 2 E4
Emmerton Rd KMP MK42 29 H1
Endsleigh Rd KMP MK42 20 D5
Engayne Av SDY/GAM/PO SG19 26 D3
Ennerdale Cl KMP MK42 29 H3
Essex Gdns KMP MK42 31 F1
Ettrick Dr BEDN MK41 14 C4
Eugster Av KMP MK42 29 G3
Everard Rd BEDN MK41 21 H1
Everton Rd SDY/GAM/PO SG19 27 H4
Evesham Abbey BEDN MK41 22 A3

F

Fairfax Rd BED MK40 20 B3
Fairholme BEDN MK41 13 H5
Fair Wy RBEDNE MK44 16 D3
Falcon Av BEDN MK41 13 E4
Falcon Cl SDY/GAM/PO SG19 26 D2
Faldo Rd KMP MK42 21 F5
Faraday Sq KMP MK42 31 E1
Farley Wy RBEDW MK43 10 A1
Farnham Wy BEDN MK41 14 A3
Farrell Rd RBEDW MK43 34 D2
Farrer St KMP MK42 30 A2
Farsands RBEDW MK43 4 D5
Faynes Ct SDY/GAM/PO SG19 27 E4
Fearnley Crs KMP MK42 30 B2
Fenlake Rd KMP MK42 3 G7
Fernlea Cl BED MK40 20 A4
Fetlock Cl BEDN MK41 11 G1
Fieldfare SDY/GAM/PO SG19 27 E1
Fieldside BEDN MK41 14 B5
Fields Rd RBEDW MK43 35 E3
Filland Ct SDY/GAM/PO SG19 26 D5
The Finches BED MK40 2 A3
SDY/GAM/PO SG19 26 D1
Finch Priory BEDN MK41 22 B3
Firbank Rd KMP MK42 21 E5
The Firs KMP MK42 30 B3
Fishers Cl RBEDNE MK44 16 C2
Fitzgerald Cl KMP MK42 21 E5
Flanders Cl KMP MK42 30 C1
Fleming Cl BED MK40 19 G2
Fontwell Cl BED MK40 3 H2
Ford End Rd BED MK40 2 A5
Foster Gv SDY/GAM/PO SG19 27 E5
Foster Hill Rd BED MK40 20 D1
Foster Pl KMP MK42 30 A2
Foster Rd KMP MK42 29 H1
RBEDW MK43 34 D1
Foster St BED MK40 2 D1
Fountains Rd BEDN MK41 13 G3
Fowler Cl BED MK40 29 H1
Foxbrook RBEDW MK43 10 A1
Foxglove Wy KMP MK42 31 G2
Foxlease BEDN MK41 13 F3
Francis Groves Cl BEDN MK41 13 F4
Franklyn Gdns BED MK40 19 G2
Fraser Rd RBEDNE MK44 22 C5
Friars Wk SDY/GAM/PO SG19 27 F3
Frome Cl BEDN MK41 13 E3
Fulmar Rd BEDN MK41 13 F4
The Furlong BEDN MK41 13 H4
Furness Cl BEDN MK41 13 H3
Furzefield BEDN MK41 13 H5

G

Gadsby St BED MK40 2 E3
Gainsborough Ri BEDN MK41 12 D5
Galloway Cl KMP MK42 29 G3
Garden Cl KMP MK42 29 H1
Gardener Pl BED MK40 19 G2
Garfield St BEDN MK41 20 D1
Garnith Cl KMP MK42 30 B2
Gateshead Cl
SDY/GAM/PO SG19 27 E2
George St BED MK40 3 J2
BEDN MK41 11 G1
Georgetown SDY/GAM/PO SG19 26 C1
Georgetown Rd
SDY/GAM/PO SG19 26 C2
Gibbons Rd BED MK40 2 B3
Gifford Rd KMP MK42 3 G7
Gilbert Cl KMP MK42 19 H5
Gillespie Cl KMP * MK42 21 E5
Gilwell Cl BEDN MK41 13 G4
Gipping Cl BEDN MK41 13 F1
Girtford Crs SDY/GAM/PO SG19 26 D4
The Glade RBEDW MK43 10 A5
Gladstone St BEDN MK41 20 D1
Glastonbury Abbey BEDN MK41 22 B3
Glebe Cl SDY/GAM/PO SG19 26 D3
Glebe Rd BED MK40 3 F1
SDY/GAM/PO SG19 27 E3
Glebe Wy AMP/FLIT/B MK45 42 C5
The Glen KMP MK42 29 H3
Glenavon Rd BEDN MK41 14 C4
Glenrose Av BEDN MK41 13 G2
Gloucester Rd KMP MK42 31 E1
Godso Cl BEDN MK41 13 H4
Godwin Cl RBEDW MK43 18 C1
Godwin Wy RBEDW MK43 18 D1
Goldcrest Wy BEDN MK41 12 D4
Goldington Av BED MK40 21 F1
Goldington Gn BEDN MK41 22 A1
Goldington Rd BED MK40 3 G2
BEDN MK41 21 H2
Gold La BED MK40 19 F2
Goodman Rd KMP MK42 30 D1
Goodmayes Cl KMP MK42 21 G5
Goodrich Av BEDN MK41 14 A4
Goodwins Yd RBEDNE MK44 17 E3
Gosforth Cl SDY/GAM/PO SG19 27 E1
Gostwick Pl RBEDNE MK44 24 A3
Gostwick Rd KMP MK42 31 E2
Gower Dr BED MK40 19 G2
Grafton Rd BED MK40 2 B3
Grange Cl AMP/FLIT/B MK45 42 C5
Grange La RBEDW MK43 10 D5
Grange Rd BEDN MK41 22 A2
Grange Wy RBEDNE MK44 24 A3
Granville St KMP MK42 2 A7
Grasmere Cl KMP MK42 30 A2
Gratton Rd BED MK40 20 B3
The Graylings BEDN MK41 13
Graze Hl RBEDNE MK44 7
Great Aldens BEDN MK41 13
Great Portway BED MK40 19
The Green RBEDW MK43 40
Greenacres BEDN MK41 13
Green End BEDN MK41 15
Green End Rd RBEDNE MK44 16
RBEDW MK43 28
Greenhill St BED MK40 2
Green La BEDN MK41 12
BEDN MK41 14
Greensand Ridge Wk
SDY/GAM/PO SG19 27
Greenshields Rd BED MK40 3
Greenview Cl KMP MK42 29
Grenidge Wy RBEDW MK43 4
Greskine Cl BEDN MK41 14
Greycote KMP MK42 32
Greyfriars BED MK40 2
The Grove AMP/FLIT/B MK45 42
BED MK40 3
Grosvenor St KMP MK42 3
Grovebury Ct RBEDW MK43 34
Grove Pl BED MK40 3
Gulliver Cl KMP MK42 29
Gunnersbury Pk BEDN MK41 22
Gwyn St BED MK40 2

H

Haden Cl BEDN MK41 12
Hadleigh Cl BEDN MK41 14
Halegate RBEDW MK43 34
Hale Ldg BED * MK40 21
Halesowen Dr KMP MK42 31
Halifax Rd KMP MK42 32
Hall End Rd RBEDW MK43 34
Hall Wy AMP/FLIT/B MK45 38
Halsey Rd KMP MK42 30
Hamble Rd BEDN MK41 13
Hammond Rd BEDN MK41 14
Hampden Ct BED MK40 19
Hampton Cl AMP/FLIT/B MK45 43
Hamsterley Cl BEDN MK41 14
Harding Cl KMP MK42 3
Hardwick Hl AMP/FLIT/B MK45 36
Hardwick Rd KMP MK42 21
Harefield Av KMP MK42 30
Harewood Rd KMP MK42 31
Hargreaves Ct KMP MK42 31
Harlech Rd BEDN MK41 13
Harpenden Cl BEDN MK41 22
Harpur St BED MK40 2
The Harriers SDY/GAM/PO SG19 26
Harrier Wy KMP MK42 30
Harrington Dr BEDN MK41 13
Harris Cl KMP MK42 30
Harrold Priory BEDN MK41 22
Harrowden La KMP MK42 31
KMP MK42 32
Harrowden Rd KMP MK42 31
Harter Rd KMP MK42 29
Hartington St BEDN MK41 20
Hartland Av BED MK40 3
Hartop Cl BEDN MK41 13
Hartshill BEDN MK41 13
Hartwell Dr KMP MK42 30
Harvey Rd BEDN MK41 22
Hassett St BED MK40 2
Hastings Rd KMP MK42 29
Hatfield Crs BEDN MK41 21
Havelock Cl SDY/GAM/PO SG19 26
Havelock St BED MK40 2
Hawk Dr BEDN MK41 12
SDY/GAM/PO SG19 26
Hawkins Rd KMP MK42 31
Hawthorne Av BED MK40 20
Hawthorne Ter RBEDW * MK43 18
Haycroft RBEDW MK43 35
Haylands Wy BEDN MK41 21
Haylock Cl KMP MK42 29
Haynes Rd KMP MK42 31
Hazelwood Rd KMP MK42 31
Heather Gdns BEDN MK41 22
Heathfield BEDN MK41 14
Helford Cl BEDN MK41 13
Helmsley Av BEDN MK41 14
Henderson Wy KMP MK42 30
Herbrand Rd KMP MK42 31
Hereford Rd KMP MK42 31
Hermitage Gdns
AMP/FLIT/B MK45 38
Heron Cl SDY/GAM/PO SG19 26
Heron Quay BED MK40 2
Heronscroft BEDN MK41 21

rons Md *RBEDW* MK43 18 D1
hbury Gv *BEDN* MK41 11 H1
ghfield Rd *KMP* MK42 30 A3
RBEDNE MK44 5 E4
gh Rd *KMP* MK42 32 B5
SDY/GAM/PO SG19 26 D5
gh St *AMP/FLIT/B* MK45 42 C5
BED MK40 2 E3
KMP MK42 29 G3
KMP MK42 30 D2
RBEDNE MK44 9 E2
RBEDNE MK44 11 G2
RBEDNE MK44 17 E3
RBEDW MK43 4 D5
SDY/GAM/PO SG19 27 E4
gh Vw *BEDN* MK41 14 A5
lesden Av *KMP* MK42 30 D2
lgrounds Rd *KMP* MK42 29 H1
Plantation *RBEDW* * MK43 18 C2
Ri *BEDN* MK41 12 D5
KMP MK42 29 F4
lson Cl *RBEDW* MK43 40 B4
ndburn Cl *BEDN* MK41 13 F2
ckley Ct *RBEDW* MK43 40 B4
ckliffe Rd *KMP* MK42 3 G7
dder Rd *BEDN* MK41 13 E1
garth Cl *BEDN* MK41 20 C1
lden Cl *BED* MK40 19 F2
e Hollies *KMP* MK42 30 B3
llies Wk *RBEDW* MK43 34 D1
llis La *RBEDNE* MK44 9 F3
lme Cl *RBEDW* MK43 40 B5
lme St *KMP* MK42 2 D6
lm Oak Gn *RBEDNE* MK44 32 D2
lt Rw *KMP* MK42 2 D6
me Cl *AMP/FLIT/B* MK45 42 C4
AMP/FLIT/B MK45 43 G1
BEDN MK41 14 B2
me Rd *RBEDW* MK43 28 D3
ney Hill Gdns *BED* MK40 20 A4
ney Hill Rd *BED* MK40 20 A4
neysuckle Wy *BEDN* MK41 22 B2
niton Wy *BED* MK40 21 G1
e Hoo *KMP* MK42 29 F4
oked La *AMP/FLIT/B* MK45 38 A4
okhams La *BEDN* MK41 14 B3
o La *RBEDW* MK43 40 C1
oper Cl *KMP* MK42 29 G4
pe Rd *KMP* MK42 30 D2
e Hornbeams *KMP* MK42 30 B3
rne La *BED* MK40 2 D4
ughton Rd *KMP* MK42 2 D7
ward Av *BED* MK40 20 B3
ward Cl *RBEDNE* MK44 33 E2
ward Pl *BED* MK40 20 B3
ward St *BED* MK40 2 E3
KMP MK42 30 B2
wbury St *BED* MK40 3 H2
wden Gdns *BED* MK40 19 G2
wes Dr *RBEDW* MK43 40 A5
ddleston Wy *BEDN* MK41 22 A3
dson Rd *BEDN* MK41 14 C5
lme Cl *KMP* MK42 30 A2
mber Av *BEDN* MK41 13 F3
nter's Cl *BEDN* MK41 11 G2
ntingdon Rd *KMP* MK42 29 H3
nts Fld *RBEDNE* MK44 16 D3
nts Pth *RBEDW* MK43 5 E5
rst Gv *BED* MK40 20 B3

I

bett Cl *RBEDW* MK43 29 E3
desleigh Rd *BED* MK40 20 B4
gham Cl *RBEDW* MK43 40 A4
gram Cl *RBEDW* MK43 40 A4
ching Cl *BEDN* MK41 13 F2
win Rd *BED* MK40 3 K2
s Rd *BEDN* MK41 13 E3
on Cl *BED* MK40 19 H2
chen Cl *BEDN* MK41 13 E3
el Cl *BEDN* MK41 13 F3
el Rd *SDY/GAM/PO* SG19 27 E5
el Vw *SDY/GAM/PO* SG19 27 F5
y La *AMP/FLIT/B* MK45 38 A5
y Rd *KMP* MK42 21 F5

J

ckman Cl *RBEDW* MK43 18 C2
mes St *BED* MK40 2 D3
smine Cl *BEDN* MK41 14 C4
e Jays *SDY/GAM/PO* SG19 27 E1
nkyn Rd *RBEDW* MK43 34 C3

John Bunyan Trail *KMP* MK42 37 H1
RBEDW MK43 4 C2
RBEDW MK43 10 B2
RBEDW MK43 18 B4
Johnson Cl *BED* MK40 19 G2
RBEDW MK43 40 A4
Jowitt Av *KMP* MK42 30 B2
Judith Gdns *KMP* MK42 29 H2

K

Kathie Rd *KMP* MK42 31 F1
Keats Cl *BED* MK40 20 B1
Keeley Farm Ct *RBEDW* MK43 28 D5
Keeley La *RBEDW* MK43 28 C5
Kelvin Av *KMP* MK42 31 E1
Kempston Rd *KMP* MK42 2 B7
Kendall Rd *KMP* MK42 29 G3
Kennedy Rd *KMP* MK42 31 E1
Kenneth Wy *AMP/FLIT/B* MK45 36 D3
Kennet Ri *BEDN* MK41 13 E2
Kent Av *KMP* MK42 31 E1
Kentmere Cl *KMP* MK42 29 H3
Kershope Cl *BEDN* MK41 14 B5
Kestrel Rd *BEDN* MK41 13 E4
Kestrel Wy *SDY/GAM/PO* SG19 26 D2
Kilpin Cl *KMP* MK42 3 H7
Kimble Dr *BEDN* MK41 22 A3
Kimbolton Av *BED* MK40 21 F1
Kimbolton Rd *BEDN* MK41 13 F5
King Edward Rd *BEDN* MK41 22 A2
Kingfisher Cl *BEDN* MK41 13 F5
SDY/GAM/PO SG19 27 E1
Kingsbrook Rd *KMP* MK42 3 F6
Kingsley Ct *SDY/GAM/PO* SG19 26 D3
Kingsley Rd *BED* MK40 3 K4
King's Pl *KMP* MK42 2 D7
King's Rd *SDY/GAM/PO* SG19 27 E4
King St *BEDN* MK41 11 H2
KMP MK42 29 H1
Kingsway *KMP* MK42 2 E6
Kingswood Cl *AMP/FLIT/B* MK45 42 D5
Kingswood Wy *BED* MK40 19 F5
King William Cl *KMP* MK42 29 G2
King William Rd *KMP* MK42 29 G3
Kirkman Cl *KMP* MK42 21 F5
Kirkstall Cl *KMP* MK42 31 E3
Kitchener Pl *RBEDW* MK43 41 H3
Kneller Cl *BEDN* MK41 12 C5
Knights Av *BEDN* MK41 11 H1

L

Laburnum Av *BED* MK40 20 B4
Laburnum Rd
SDY/GAM/PO SG19 26 D4
Lakeview *RBEDW* MK43 40 C3
Lambourn Wy *BEDN* MK41 13 F2
Lancaster Av *KMP* MK42 31 E2
Lancaster Rd *KMP* MK42 31 H4
Lanchester Cl *BEDN* MK41 12 A2
Landseer Wk *BEDN* MK41 20 C1
Langdale *BEDN* MK41 13 G5
Lansdowne Rd *BED* MK40 2 A1
The Larches *KMP* MK42 30 B3
Larks Ri *SDY/GAM/PO* SG19 27 E1
Larkway *BEDN* MK41 13 F4
Laural Wk *KMP* MK42 30 B3
Lavenham Dr *BED* MK40 19 G2
Lawrence St *BED* MK40 20 B4
Laycock Abbey *BEDN* MK41 22 B3
Leasway *BEDN* MK41 13 H5
Lee Cl *BED* MK40 19 G2
Leeds Smith Dr
SDY/GAM/PO SG19 27 E4
Leighfield Cl *BEDN* MK41 14 C5
Leith Rd *KMP* MK42 31 H1
Lely Cl *BEDN* MK41 12 C5
Ley Side *RBEDW* MK43 18 D1
Lichfield Cl *KMP* MK42 30 A1
Lilac Wk *KMP* MK42 30 B3
Lilleshall Dr *KMP* MK42 31 E3
Lily Cl *KMP* MK42 31 H2
Lime Av *SDY/GAM/PO* SG19 26 D5
Lime Cl *RBEDW* MK43 18 C2
Lime St *BED* MK40 2 D3
Lincoln Rd *KMP* MK42 29 H4
KMP MK42 32 A4
Lincroft *RBEDW* MK43 5 E5
Linden Rd *BED* MK40 20 C1
Lindisfarne Cl
SDY/GAM/PO SG19 27 E3
Lindisfarne Priory *BEDN* MK41 22 B3
The Links *KMP* MK42 30 A3

Linkway *BEDN* MK41 22 A1
Linnet Wy *BEDN* MK41 13 E4
Littledale St *KMP* MK42 30 B1
Little Grove Pl *BED* MK40 3 F3
Little Headlands *BEDN* MK41 13 H4
Little Portway *BED* MK40 19 F5
Little Townsend Cl *KMP* MK42 30 D2
Lodge Av *KMP* MK42 29 G3
Lombardy Cl *BEDN* MK41 13 F4
London La *AMP/FLIT/B* MK45 42 D5
London Rd *KMP* MK42 21 F5
SDY/GAM/PO SG19 26 C3
Longfield Rd *SDY/GAM/PO* SG19 26 D3
Longholme Wy *KMP* MK42 3 H6
Longleat *BEDN* MK41 22 C2
Lorraine Rd *RBEDW* MK43 34 C2
Lovat Wk *KMP* MK42 30 B3
Lovell Rd *KMP* MK42 31 H1
RBEDW MK43 11 F2
Loveridge Av *KMP* MK42 29 H1
Lower Farm Rd *RBEDW* MK43 11 F4
Lower Shelton Rd *RBEDW* MK43 40 A2
Lowther Rd *BEDN* MK41 13 G3
Lucas Ct *BED* MK40 19 G2
Luke Pl *KMP* MK42 31 E2
Lurke St *BED* MK40 2 E3
Luton Rd *AMP/FLIT/B* MK45 37 G5
Lydford Cl *BED* MK40 3 K1
Lymington Gdns *BEDN* MK41 14 C4
Lynn Cl *KMP* MK42 31 E4
Lynton Gv *KMP* MK42 30 D2
Lyon Cl *KMP* MK42 30 A4
Lytham Pl *BED* MK40 19 F5

M

Mabel Rd *KMP* MK42 30 D1
Magnolia Cl *KMP* MK42 30 B4
Main Rd *BED* MK40 19 G3
Maitland St *BED* MK40 2 C4
Malakand Rd *KMP* MK42 30 C1
Malaunay Pl *SDY/GAM/PO* SG19 27 E4
Malcote Cl *BED* MK40 19 G2
Mallard Hl *BEDN* MK41 13 E4
Malmesbury Abbey *BEDN* MK41 22 A3
Maltings Wy *RBEDNE* MK44 16 D3
Malvern Av *BEDN* MK41 21 H1
Manorbier Rd *BEDN* MK41 13 H3
Manor Cl *KMP* MK42 29 H2
RBEDNE MK44 9 F2
RBEDW MK43 11 E4
Manor Ct *RBEDW* * MK43 40 A5
Manor Dr *KMP* MK42 29 H2
Manor Pk *KMP* * MK42 31 F1
Manor Rd *BED* MK40 19 F3
BEDN MK41 22 A1
RBEDW MK43 35 E2
RBEDW MK43 40 A5
SDY/GAM/PO SG19 26 D3
Manor Wy *AMP/FLIT/B* MK45 38 D2
Manton La *BEDN* MK41 12 C5
Manton Lane Rbt *BEDN* MK41 20 C1
Maple Rd *SDY/GAM/PO* SG19 27 E2
The Maples *KMP* MK42 30 A3
Mardale Cl *KMP* MK42 30 A2
Mareth Rd *KMP* MK42 21 G5
Margetts Rd *KMP* MK42 30 B2
Marigold Wy *KMP* MK42 31 G2
Marina Ct *KMP* MK42 2 A7
Market Sq *SDY/GAM/PO* SG19 27 E4
Mark Rutherford Rd *KMP* MK42 21 F5
Marlborough Pk *KMP* MK42 20 B5
Marlborough Rd *BED* MK40 20 B3
Marlow Wy *BEDN* MK41 13 E2
Marne St *KMP* MK42 20 C5
Marshall Cl *BED* MK40 29 H1
Marshall Ct *BEDN* MK41 22 A2
Martin Cl *BEDN* MK41 13 F4
Maryville Rd *KMP* MK42 30 D1
Massey Cl *KMP* MK42 30 A2
Mayfield Cl *KMP* MK42 30 A1
Mayfield Ct *SDY/GAM/PO* SG19 26 D4
Mayhew Cl *RBEDW* MK43 18 C2
Meadow La *RBEDNE* MK44 22 D4
The Meadows *RBEDW* MK43 41 G3
Meadowsweet Dr *KMP* MK42 31 G2
Meadowview Rd *KMP* MK42 29 G2
Meadway *BEDN* MK41 22 A1
Medbury La *KMP* MK42 31 E4
Medusa Wy *SDY/GAM/PO* SG19 26 D2
Meeting Cl *AMP/FLIT/B* MK45 38 D2
Melbourne St *KMP* MK42 2 D6
Melrose Dr *KMP* MK42 31 E3
Mendip Crs *BEDN* MK41 21 G1
Mentmore Cl *BED* MK40 19 F5
Mepham Rd *RBEDW* MK43 34 D1

Merlin Dr *SDY/GAM/PO* SG19 26 D1
Merlin Gdns *BEDN* MK41 13 E4
Merton Rd *BED* MK40 3 G1
Middleham Cl
SDY/GAM/PO SG19 27 E3
Midland Rd *BED* MK40 2 C4
SDY/GAM/PO SG19 26 D3
Midway *RBEDW* * MK43 4 C1
Milburn Rd *BEDN* MK41 14 B4
Mile Rd *KMP* MK42 31 F2
Millbrook Rd *KMP* MK42 20 D5
Miller Rd *KMP* MK42 30 D1
Millfield *RBEDW* MK43 18 D1
Mill La *AMP/FLIT/B* MK45 42 D4
KMP MK42 29 G2
SDY/GAM/PO SG19 26 D5
Mill St *BED* MK40 2 E3
Mills Wk *SDY/GAM/PO* SG19 27 E3
Milne Rw *BED* MK40 20 B2
Milton Rd *BED* MK40 20 B2
BEDN MK41 5 G5
Mitford Cl *BEDN* MK41 14 A4
Mitre Cl *BEDN* MK41 22 B2
Molivers La *RBEDW* MK43 10 D5
Monkshill *BEDN* MK41 22 A1
Monmouth Cl *KMP* MK42 31 F1
Monoux Pl *SDY/GAM/PO* SG19 27 E4
Monoux Rd *RBEDW* MK43 35 E3
Montgomery Cl *RBEDW* MK43 41 G3
Moor La *KMP* MK42 31 F2
Moreteyne Rd *RBEDW* MK43 40 A4
Morgans Cl *AMP/FLIT/B* MK45 43 H1
Moriston Rd *BEDN* MK41 13 E2
Mortimer Rd *KMP* MK42 19 H5
Moss La *KMP* MK42 31 E5
Moulton Av *KMP* MK42 21 G5
Mountbatten Pl *BEDN* MK41 22 A2
Mount Dr *BEDN* MK41 14 A5
Mount Pleasant Rd *BEDN* MK41 11 H2
Mowbray Cl *RBEDW* MK43 10 C5
Mowbray Pl *RBEDNE* MK44 24 A2
Mowbray Rd *KMP* MK42 31 E2
Mowsbury Pk *BEDN* * MK41 13 G2
Mulberry Wk *KMP* MK42 30 B3
Muirfield *BED* MK40 19 F5
Murdock Rd *BEDN* MK41 12 C4
Muswell Rd *KMP* MK42 30 D1
Myrtle Rd *KMP* MK42 31 F1

N

Napier Rd *BEDN* MK41 14 D5
Nash Rd *KMP* MK42 21 G5
Naylor Av *KMP* MK42 29 H4
Neale Rd *RBEDW* MK43 34 D1
Neath Abbey *BEDN* MK41 22 B3
Needwood Rd *BEDN* MK41 14 B5
Nelson St *BED* MK40 20 B4
Nevern Gdns *BED* MK40 19 G2
Neville Crs *RBEDW* MK43 18 C1
Newark Av *BEDN* MK41 14 A3
Newbury Cl *KMP* MK42 29 H2
New Cl *RBEDNE* MK44 7 H4
Newnham Av *BEDN* MK41 3 K5
Newnham Rd *BED* MK40 3 F4
Newnham St *BED* MK40 3 F3
New Rd *RBEDNE* MK44 17 F3
RBEDW MK43 18 C2
Newstead Wy *BEDN* MK41 13 H3
Newton Rd *KMP* MK42 31 E1
Newton Wy *SDY/GAM/PO* SG19 27 E3
Nicholls Cl *RBEDW* MK43 40 A4
Nicholls Rd *KMP* MK42 3 H7
Nightingale Av *BEDN* MK41 13 E3
Nodders Wy *BED* MK40 19 G2
Norfolk Cl *BEDN* MK41 13 F2
Norman Cl *RBEDNE* MK44 16 D3
Normandy Cl *KMP* MK42 30 B1
Norse Rd *BEDN* MK41 14 B4
Northampton Rd *RBEDW* MK43 10 A5
Northcote *BEDN* MK41 14 A5
Northcroft *SDY/GAM/PO* SG19 27 E4
Northdale Cl *KMP* MK42 30 C2
North Dr *KMP* MK42 32 A3
Northill Rd *RBEDNE* MK44 33 H2
North Pde *BED* * MK40 2 C2
North Vw *RBEDW* * MK43 18 C2
Northway Ct *KMP* MK42 3 G7
Northwood La
AMP/FLIT/B MK45 38 A5
Nursery Dr *SDY/GAM/PO* SG19 26 C3
Nursery Gdns *BEDN* MK41 13 F5
Nutwood Cl *BEDN* MK41 14 C5

O

Oak Cl *RBEDW* MK43 35 E1
SDY/GAM/PO SG19 26 D3
Oaklands Rd *BED* MK40 21 F1
Oakley Rd *BEDN* MK41 11 G2
RBEDW MK43 10 D3
Oak Rd *KMP* MK42 31 F1
Odell Cl *KMP* MK42 19 H5
Odin Cl *BEDN* MK41 14 D4
Offa Rd *KMP* MK42 20 D5
Oldfield Rd *BED* MK40 20 A4
Old Ford End Rd *BED* MK40 19 H4
Old Harrowden Rd *KMP* MK42 31 H3
Old Station Ct *RBEDNE* MK44 25 H1
Oldways Rd *RBEDNE* MK44 7 H4
Ombersley Rd *KMP* MK42 2 C7
Ongley Ct *SDY/GAM/PO* * SG19 27 F5
Onley Ct *SDY/GAM/PO* SG19 27 F5
Orchard Cl *BEDN* MK41 13 G5
RBEDW MK43 10 D5
Orchard St *KMP* MK42 30 A3
Orchard Wy *RBEDNE* MK44 17 E4
RBEDW * MK43 18 C2
Ormesby Wy *BED* MK40 20 A4
Orwell Cl *BEDN* MK41 13 E3
Osprey Cl *KMP* MK42 30 A4
Ossory Wy *KMP* MK42 20 D5
Ouseland Rd *BED* MK40 20 A4
Ouse Rd *BEDN* MK41 22 A1
Overdale *BEDN* MK41 14 A5
Owen Cl *KMP* MK42 29 G3
RBEDW MK43 40 A4

P

Paddock Cl *BEDN* MK41 11 H1
The Paddocks *RBEDW* MK43 18 D2
Palmerston St *BEDN* MK41 20 C1
Paradine Rd *KMP* MK42 21 F5
Park Av *BED* MK40 21 E1
Park Cl *RBEDNE* MK44 25 F5
Park Ct *SDY/GAM/PO* SG19 27 E5
Park Crs *RBEDW* MK43 41 G3
Parkland *RBEDW* MK43 10 B5
Parklands *BEDN* MK41 21 H1
Park Rd *KMP* MK42 30 B1
RBEDNE MK44 25 F5
RBEDW MK43 10 A1
SDY/GAM/PO SG19 27 E4
Park Rd North *BEDN* MK41 20 D1
Park Rd West *BEDN* MK41 20 C1
Parkside *RBEDNE* MK44 5 F1
Parkstone Cl *BEDN* MK41 13 G2
Park Vw *RBEDNE* MK44 17 H5
Parrish Cl *RBEDW* MK43 40 B4
Parsonage Cl *RBEDW* MK43 11 E1
Partridge Piece
SDY/GAM/PO SG19 26 D1
Partridge La *RBEDW* MK43 18 B2
The Pastures *RBEDW* MK43 41 G3
Paula Radcliffe Wy
(Clapham By-Pass)
RBEDW MK43 11 G3
Paul Waller Av *KMP* MK42 32 B2
Pavenham Rd *RBEDW* MK43 4 A1
Pax Hl *BEDN* MK41 13 G4
Payne Rd *RBEDW* MK43 34 D2
Pearcey Rd *KMP* MK42 31 E1
Pearmain Cl *BEDN* MK41 21 H2
Pear Tree Cl *RBEDW* MK43 18 B2
Pear Tree Vw *KMP* MK42 31 E4
Peashill La *RBEDNE* MK44 16 D2
Peel's Pl *SDY/GAM/PO* SG19 27 F4
Pemberley Av *BED* MK40 21 E1
Pemberley La *BED* MK40 3 F1
Pembroke Cl *RBEDW* MK43 40 B4
Pembroke Rd *AMP/FLIT/B* MK45 42 D5
Pembroke St *BED* MK40 3 H3
Pendennis Rd *BEDN* MK41 14 A4
Penlee Cl *BEDN* MK41 21 H2
Pennine Rd *BEDN* MK41 13 G5
Pentland Cl *SDY/GAM/PO* SG19 26 D3
Pentland Ri *BEDN* MK41 13 G5
Penwright Cl *KMP* MK42 29 H1
Perkins Rd *BEDN* MK41 22 C1
Pershore Cl *BEDN* MK41 13 G3
Pevensey Rd *BEDN* MK41 14 B5
Phillpotts Av *BED* MK40 3 K2
Phipps Cl *AMP/FLIT/B* MK45 43 H1
Pickering Cl *SDY/GAM/PO* SG19 27 E3
Pilcroft St *KMP* MK42 2 E6
Pilgrims Cl *KMP* MK42 31 E2
Pilgrims Wy *KMP* MK42 31 E2
Pillinge Rd *RBEDW* MK43 41 G3
The Pines *KMP* MK42 30 B3
Pinsent Av *RBEDW* MK43 18 C2
Pipit Gv *SDY/GAM/PO* SG19 26 D2
Pipit Ri *BEDN* MK41 13 E4
The Planes *KMP* MK42 30 A3
Plover Wy *BEDN* MK41 12 D4
Polhill Av *BEDN* MK41 21 G1
Pollards Cl *AMP/FLIT/B* MK45 43 G1
Polo Field Wy
AMP/FLIT/B MK45 30 B4
Poplar Av *BEDN* MK41 13 G3
Poplar Gv *SDY/GAM/PO* SG19 26 C4
Poppyfields *BEDN* MK41 14 C4
Portland Cl *BEDN* MK41 22 A1
Postley Rd *KMP* MK42 29 H4
Potters Cross *RBEDW* MK43 35 E2
Potter Wy *KMP* MK42 31 E2
Potton Rd *SDY/GAM/PO* SG19 27 H5
Poulter Cl *BED* MK40 2 C5
Powers Cl *SDY/GAM/PO* SG19 26 D2
Powis Rd *BEDN* MK41 14 B4
Prebend St *BED* MK40 2 C4
Prentice Gdns *KMP* MK42 30 B1
Preston Rd *BED* MK40 20 B3
Prestwick Rd *BED* MK40 19 F4
Primrose Cl *RBEDW* MK43 40 A5
Princes Rd *RBEDW* MK43 18 C1
Princess St *BEDN* MK41 11 H2
Princes St *BED* MK40 2 D1
Prinknash Rd *BEDN* MK41 13 G3
Priory St *BED* MK40 2 C3
Proctor Cl *KMP* MK42 29 H1
Progress Wy *KMP* MK42 30 D2
Prudden Cl *KMP* MK42 30 D2
Purbeck Cl *BEDN* MK41 22 A1
Putnoe Hts *BEDN* MK41 13 H4
Putnoe La *BEDN* MK41 13 G5
Putnoe St *BEDN* MK41 14 A4
Pyms Cl *RBEDNE* MK44 16 D3
Pym's Wy *SDY/GAM/PO* SG19 26 D2

Q

Quantock Cl *BEDN* MK41 21 G1
Quantrelle Ct *KMP* MK42 32 A3
Queen Alexandra Rd
BEDN MK41 22 A2
Queensbury Cl *BED* MK40 20 B3
Queen's Cl *BED* MK40 19 H2
RBEDW MK43 4 D5
Queens Crs *BEDN* MK41 11 H2
BEDN MK41 13 H5
Queen's Dr *BEDN* MK41 13 H4
Queen's Rd *SDY/GAM/PO* SG19 26 D4
Queen St *BED* MK40 2 C1
Quenby Wy *RBEDW* MK43 18 D2
Quince Ct *SDY/GAM/PO* * SG19 26 D2

R

Raglan Gn *BEDN* MK41 14 A4
Railton Rd *RBEDW* MK43 29 H5
Raleigh St *BED* MK40 20 B4
Ramillies Cl *KMP* MK42 30 B1
Ramsay Cl *BEDN* MK41 12 D5
Ramsey Cl *KMP* MK42 29 H4
Randalls Cl *RBEDW* MK43 18 D1
Ravensden Rd *BEDN* MK41 14 A1
RBEDNE MK44 8 D2
Ray's Cl *KMP* MK42 3 F5
Rectory Ct *SDY/GAM/PO* * SG19 27 F4
Rectory La *AMP/FLIT/B* MK45 42 C5
Red Cedar Rd *RBEDW* MK43 10 A4
Reddall Cl *KMP* MK42 31 H1
Rede Cl *BEDN* MK41 13 E2
Redwald Cl *KMP* MK42 30 A3
Redwood Gv *KMP* MK42 3 F7
Regent Cl *BEDN* MK41 13 E2
Regents Ms *BED* MK40 19 G2
Renhold Rd *RBEDNE* MK44 9 E4
Repton Cl *BEDN* MK41 13 H4
Restormel Cl *BEDN* MK41 13 H3
Reynes Cl *RBEDW* MK43 40 B5
Reynes Dr *RBEDW* MK43 5 E5
Reynolds Cl *BEDN* MK41 20 C1
Rhineland Wy *BEDN* MK41 13 F2
Ribble Wy *BEDN* MK41 13 E2
Richbell Ct *BED* MK40 2 C1
Richmond Rd *BED* MK40 3 H1
Ridge Rd *RBEDW* MK43 29 E4
The Ridgeway *BEDN* MK41 14 A4
RBEDNE MK44 26 A4
Ridgmount St *KMP* MK42 20 D5
Ringwood Cl *KMP* MK42 30 B2
Ripon Cl *KMP* MK42 20 A5
Risborough Rd *BEDN* MK41 21 H2
The Risings *BEDN* MK41 14 A5
Riverfield Dr *BEDN* MK41 22 A3
River La *RBEDNE* MK44 5 F1
Rivermead Gdns
SDY/GAM/PO SG19 26 D4
Riverside Cl *KMP* MK42 2 A7
River St *BED* MK40 2 C4
Riverview *RBEDW* * MK43 4 C1
Riverview Wy *KMP* MK42 29 G2
Roberts Dr *RBEDW* MK43 40 C2
Robin Cl *SDY/GAM/PO* SG19 26 D2
Robin Hl *BEDN* MK41 13 E4
Roff Av *BED* MK40 2 C1
Roise St *BED* MK40 2 C2
Roman Vw *SDY/GAM/PO* SG19 27 F5
Romsey Wy *KMP* MK42 31 E3
Ronald Cl *KMP* MK42 30 A4
The Rookery *SDY/GAM/PO* SG19 27 E1
Rooksmead *BEDN* MK41 13 E4
Rope Wk *KMP* MK42 3 G6
Rosamond Rd *BED* MK40 3 J2
Roseby Wy *BEDN* MK41 22 A3
Rose Crs *RBEDW* * MK43 4 C1
Rosedale Wy *KMP* MK42 30 A2
Rosemary Dr *RBEDW* MK43 18 C1
Rose Wk *RBEDW* * MK43 18 C2
Rothbury Cl *SDY/GAM/PO* SG19 27 E1
Rother Cl *BEDN* MK41 13 F3
Rothsay Gdns *BED* MK40 3 G2
Rothsay Pl *BED* MK40 3 G3
Roundmead *BEDN* MK41 14 A5
Rousbury Rd *RBEDW* MK43 41 G3
Rowallan Dr *BEDN* MK41 13 G3
Rowan Ct *SDY/GAM/PO* SG19 26 D3
The Rowans *KMP* MK42 30 B3
Rowlandson Wy *BEDN* MK41 12 C5
Roxton Rd *RBEDNE* MK44 16 D3
Ruffs Furze *RBEDW* MK43 10 D1
Rush Ct *BED* MK40 3 F2
Russell Av *BED* MK40 3 J4
Russell Dr *RBEDNE* MK44 24 A3
Russell Wy *RBEDW* MK43 34 D3
Russet Cl *RBEDW* MK43 41 F3
Rutland Gdns
SDY/GAM/PO SG19 27 E4
Rutland Rd *BED* MK40 2 B3
Rye Crs *RBEDNE* MK44 23 G5
Ryswick Rd *KMP* MK42 30 C1
Ryton Cl *BEDN* MK41 13 E2

S

Saddle Cl *BEDN* MK41 11 G1
Saffron Cl *BED* MK40 2 C3
St Alban Rd *BED* MK40 13 F5
St Andrews Rd *BED* MK40 21 E1
St Augustine's Rd *BED* MK40 13 F5
St Cuthbert's St *BED* MK40 3 F2
St Edmond Rd *BED* MK40 21 F1
St George's Rd *BED* MK40 21 E1
St Helena Rd *KMP* MK42 31 F1
St Helenas Gdn *KMP* MK42 30 D2
St John's Av *KMP* MK42 29 H3
St Johns Homes *KMP* * MK42 29 H2
St John's Rd *RBEDNE* MK44 25 F5
St John's St *KMP* MK42 2 E5
KMP MK42 29 H3
St Leonard's Av *KMP* MK42 2 E7
St Leonard's St *KMP* MK42 2 E6
St Loyes St *BED* MK40 2 D2
St Martins Ct *KMP* * MK42 32 A1
St Martins Wy *KMP* MK42 32 A1
St Marys Cl *KMP* MK42 30 C2
RBEDW MK43 40 B5
St Marys Rd *RBEDW* MK43 34 C2
St Mary's St *KMP* MK42 2 E4
St Mathews Cl *KMP* MK42 29 H3
St Mellion Dr *BED* MK40 19 F4
St Michael's Rd *BED* MK40 21 E1
St Minver Rd *BED* MK40 21 F1
St Neots Rd *BEDN* MK41 15 F5
SDY/GAM/PO SG19 26 D3
St Paul's Rd *BED* MK40 20 B4
St Paul's Sq *BED* MK40 2 D4
St Peter's St *BED* MK40 2 E2
St Swithun's Wy
SDY/GAM/PO SG19 27 E4
Salcombe Cl *BED* MK40 3 K1
Salisbury St *BEDN* MK41 20 D1
Saltash Cl *BED* MK40 21 G1
Sanders Cl *KMP* MK42 19 H5
Sandford Ri *SDY/GAM/PO* SG19 26 C4
Sandhurst Pl *KMP* MK42 20 D5
Sandhurst Rd *KMP* MK42 20
Sand La *SDY/GAM/PO* SG19 27
Sandon Cl *SDY/GAM/PO* SG19 27
Sandy Rd *BEDN* MK41 22
RBEDNE MK44 24
Saunders Gdns *BED* MK40 20
Savannah Cl *KMP* MK42 30
Saville Cl *RBEDNE* MK44 17
School La *RBEDNE* MK44 17
Scotchbrook Rd *RBEDW* MK43 40
Scott Av *KMP* MK42 32
Seaton Dr *BED* MK40 3
Selsey Wy *BEDN* MK41 21
Sergeants Wy *BEDN* MK41 22
Severn Wy *BEDN* MK41 13
Sexton Av *KMP* MK42 30
Shaftesbury Av *BED* MK40 3
Shakespeare Rd *BED* MK40 20
Shaldon Ct *BED* MK40 21
Shannon Cl *SDY/GAM/PO* SG19 26
Shearley Cl *BED* MK40 20
Short St *BED* MK40 20
Shrubbery La *RBEDNE* MK44 8
Shuttleworth Rd *BEDN* MK41 14
Sibton Abbey *BEDN* MK41 22
Sidmouth Cl *BED* MK40 21
Sidney Rd *BED* MK40 20
The Silver Birches *KMP* MK42 30
Silverdale St *KMP* MK42 30
Silver St *BED* MK40 2
RBEDNE MK44 16
Singer Wy *KMP* MK42 29
Skipton Cl *SDY/GAM/PO* SG19 27
The Slade *BEDN* MK41 12
Slade Wk *BEDN* MK41 20
Slater Cl *KMP* MK42 29
Snagge Ct *RBEDW* MK43 40
Somerton Cl *BEDN* MK41 13
Sopwith Wy *KMP* MK42 32
South Av *KMP* MK42 31
South Dr *KMP* MK42 32
Southfields Rd *KMP* MK42 30
Southill Rd *RBEDNE* MK44 32
RBEDNE MK44 39
South Rd *SDY/GAM/PO* SG19 26
South Rbt *BED* MK40 12
Southview *RBEDW* * MK43 18
Southville Rd *KMP* MK42 30
Southway *KMP* MK42 31
Sovereigns Quay *BED* MK40 2
Spencer Rd *SDY/GAM/PO* SG19 27
The Spencers *RBEDNE* MK44 17
Spenser Rd *BED* MK40 20
The Spinney *BEDN* MK41 14
RBEDW * MK43 11
RBEDW * MK43 18
Springfield Av *KMP* MK42 30
Springfield Dr *RBEDW* MK43 10
Spring Gdns *KMP* MK42 30
Spring Gv *SDY/GAM/PO* SG19 26
Spring Rd *KMP* MK42 30
Spruce Wk *KMP* MK42 30
The Square *AMP/FLIT/B* MK45 37
Squires Rd *RBEDW* MK43 34
RBEDW MK43 40
Stables Ct *RBEDW* * MK43 35
Stafford Rd *KMP* MK42 20
Stagsden Rd *RBEDW* MK43 18
Stainmore Rd *BEDN* MK41 14
Stanbridge Wy
AMP/FLIT/B MK45 42
Stancliffe Rd *BEDN* MK41 13
Stanhope Rd *BEDN* MK41 13
Stanley St *BEDN* MK41 20
KMP MK42 30
Stannard Wy *RBEDNE* MK44 22
Stanton Rd *KMP* MK42 29
Stapleton Rd *KMP* MK42 31
Starling Cl *SDY/GAM/PO* SG19 26
Starling Wy *BEDN* MK41 13
Station Rd *KMP* MK42 2
RBEDNE MK44 24
RBEDNE MK44 25
RBEDW MK43 5
RBEDW MK43 40
SDY/GAM/PO SG19 27
Stewartby Wy *RBEDW* MK43 41
Stewart Cl *RBEDW* MK43 11
Stewart Ct *RBEDW* MK43 35
Stirling Cl *SDY/GAM/PO* SG19 26
Stirling Rd *KMP* MK42 31
Stockton End
SDY/GAM/PO SG19 27
Stoke Albany Ms *BED* * MK40 2
Stokesay Cl *BEDN* MK41 14
Stone Cl *BED* MK40 19
Stonecroft *SDY/GAM/PO* SG19 27
Stonedale Rd *KMP* MK42 30

one Pine Rd RBEDW MK43 ....10 B5
our Wy BEDN MK41 ....13 E3
ratford Rd SDY/GAM/PO SG19.....27 F5
ratford Wy RBEDW MK43 ....40 B2
rathconon Rd BEDN MK41 ....14 C4
ratton Wy BEDN MK41 ....14 D5
uart Rd KMP MK42.......................30 A2
udley Rd RBEDW MK43 ....34 C2
immerfield Dr RBEDW MK43 ......34 D3
inbeam Rd KMP MK42..................29 H4
inderland Cl RBEDNE MK44............7 H4
inderland Hl RBEDNE MK44 ....8 A2
inderland Pl KMP MK42................32 A4
inderland Rd
SDY/GAM/PO SG19.......................27 E2
vaden SDY/GAM/PO SG19..............27 G5
van La SDY/GAM/PO SG19...........26 D5
vansholme Gdns
SDY/GAM/PO SG19.......................26 D5
vift Cl BEDN MK41........................12 D4
SDY/GAM/PO SG19.......................27 E1
vindale BEDN MK41 ....13 F2
bil's Wy AMP/FLIT/B MK45.........42 C4
e Sycamores KMP MK42..............30 B3
monds Cl RBEDW MK43 ....18 D2

T

lbot Rd BED MK40 ....3 K1
lisman Cl SDY/GAM/PO SG19 ......26 D2
mar Rd BEDN MK41......................13 F3
mworth Rd BEDN MK41 ....13 H3
ndys Cl RBEDW MK43 ....4 A1
unton Cl BEDN MK41...................14 A3
vistock Pl BED MK40.....................2 C2
vistock St BED MK40.....................2 C1
fford Wy KMP MK42.....................32 B1
mpsford St KMP MK42 ....30 A2
nnyson Rd BED MK40 ....3 K4
st Cl BEDN MK41..........................13 F1
wkesbury Rd KMP MK42 ....31 F3
etford Cl KMP MK42 ....30 B2
ickthorn La
AMP/FLIT/B MK45.........................42 B1
irlmere Rd KMP MK42..................29 H2
istley La RBEDW MK43 ....18 C1
omson Av KMP MK42 ....32 A4
or Dr BEDN MK41........................14 D5
ornton St KMP MK42 ....30 B2
orpe Cl BED MK40 ....19 F2
reave Cl BEDN MK41 ....13 H3
urleigh Rd RBEDNE MK44..............7 G2
urlestone Cl BED MK40................21 H2
urlow St BED MK40........................2 C3
urne Wy BEDN MK41....................13 F1
nsley Cl BEDN MK41 ....11 G1
ntern Abbey BEDN MK41..............22 A3
tchfield Dr KMP MK42 ....31 E3
pcat Cl KMP MK42........................30 D2
the Barn Rd RBEDW MK43 ....34 D2
Tithe Rd RBEDW MK43 ....28 C4
Tiverton Rd BED MK40 ....21 F1
Tollgate Cl RBEDW MK43 ....18 C2
Top End BEDN MK41 ....15 E2
Torre Abbey BEDN MK41 ....22 B3
Torridge Ri BEDN MK41...................13 E3
Totnes Cl BED MK40..........................3 K1
Town Cl AMP/FLIT/B MK45.............37 G5
Trent Rd BEDN MK41 ....13 F3
Trevor Dr RBEDW MK43 ....18 C1
Trevor St BED MK40..........................2 B2
Trinity Gdns BED * MK40..................2 C2
Trinity Rd BED MK40 ....20 B4
Triumph Wy KMP MK42 ....30 A4
Troon Cl BEDN MK41 ....13 G3
Trow Cl AMP/FLIT/B MK45 ....38 C2
Tudor Cl BED MK40 ....2 A1
RBEDW MK43..................................10 D5
Tulip Tree Cl RBEDW MK43 ....10 A5
Turner Wy BEDN MK41 ....12 C5
Turnpike Wy BEDN MK41 ....14 B5
Tweedsmuir Rd BEDN MK41 ....13 H4
Twinwood Rd BEDN MK41 ....11 G1
Tylecote Cl RBEDW MK43 ....40 A5
Tyne Crs BEDN MK41 ....13 E2
Tyne Rd SDY/GAM/PO SG19 ....27 E1

U

Ullswater Cl KMP MK42....................30 A3
Union St BED MK40 ....2 B2
Uplands BEDN MK41 ....13 H4
Ursula Taylor Wk BEDN MK41 ....12 A3

V

Vanguard Cl KMP MK42 ....19 H5
Vicarage Cl RBEDNE MK44 ....8 B4
Vicarage La AMP/FLIT/B MK45 ......43 G1
Vicars Cl BED MK40 ....19 G3
Vicars Wk BEDN MK41......................22 B1
Victoria Dr AMP/FLIT/B MK45 ....42 C4
Victoria Rd KMP MK42 ....2 B7
Viking Gv KMP MK42 ....19 H5
Village Rd RBEDW MK43...................10 D5
Vineyard Wy KMP MK42...................30 A1
Violet Cl KMP MK42 ....31 H2
Voyce Wy KMP MK42 ....21 F5
Vulcan St KMP MK42 ....21 E5
Vyne Cl BED MK40 ....29 H1

W

Wagstaffe Cl BEDN MK41.................13 G2
Walcourt Rd KMP MK42 ....30 B1
Walnut Cl RBEDNE MK44 ....17 H5
RBEDW MK43.................................18 B2
Walnut Wk KMP MK42 ....30 B3
Waltham Cl BEDN MK41 ....13 H3
Waltham Dr KMP MK42 ....31 F3
Wansbeck Rd BEDN MK41 ....13 E3
Warden Abbey BEDN MK41 ....22 B2
Warkworth Cl
SDY/GAM/PO SG19........................27 E3
The Warren BEDN MK41 ....12 A3
Warwick Av BED MK40 ....20 C1
Washburn Cl BEDN MK41 ....13 F2
Water End BEDN MK41 ....15 G4
RBEDNE MK44 ....33 H2
Water La KMP MK42 ....29 G3
Waterloo Rd BED MK40 ....3 F4
Watson Rd AMP/FLIT/B MK45 ....36 D3
Wavell Cl RBEDW MK43...................41 H3
Waveney Av BEDN MK41 ....13 E4
Waverly Av SDY/GAM/PO SG19 ......26 D2
The Wear BEDN MK41 ....13 E1
Weaver Cl BEDN MK41 ....13 F2
Weavers Gn SDY/GAM/PO SG19 ....27 E1
Webbs Cl RBEDW MK43...................18 D1
Wedgwood Rd BEDN MK41 ....12 D5
Welbeck Gdns BEDN MK41.............13 H3
Wellington Rd KMP MK42 ....31 H4
Wellington St BED MK40 ....2 D1
Wells Cl KMP MK42 ....20 A5
Wendover Dr BEDN MK41 ....21 H2
Wenlock Rd KMP MK42...................29 G3
Wentworth Dr BEDN MK41 ....14 B3
Wesley Rd SDY/GAM/PO SG19........27 E3
Westbourne Rd BED MK40.............20 B3
Westdale Wk KMP MK42 ....30 B2
West End AMP/FLIT/B MK45 ....30 D3
West End Rd RBEDW MK43 ....28 A2
Western St BED MK40.......................2 C4
Western Wy
SDY/GAM/PO SG19........................26 D3
Westfield Rd BED MK40 ....20 B3
RBEDW MK43...................................4 A4
West Gv BED * MK40 ....20 B2
Westminster Gdns KMP MK42........30 A1
West Rd SDY/GAM/PO SG19............26 D3
Westrope Wy BEDN MK41 ....13 F1
West Vw RBEDW * MK43.................18 C2
West Wy RBEDNE MK44 ....25 G4
Westwood Cl KMP MK42 ....32 A4
Wheathouse Cl BEDN MK41............13 H3
Whitbread Av KMP MK42 ....2 A7
Whitby Wy KMP MK42 ....31 E3
White Beam Cl KMP MK42 ....30 B4
White Lodge Cl KMP MK42.............29 G3
Whitings BED MK40.........................19 F5
Whitley Rd KMP MK42 ....32 A3
Whittingstall Av KMP MK42............30 B2
Whitworth Wy
AMP/FLIT/B MK45..........................43 H1
Widecombe Cl BED MK40...............21 G1
Wigram Cl KMP MK42 ....30 D2
Wilden Rd BEDN MK41 ....14 C1
Wildflower Wy KMP MK42 ....31 H2
Williamson Rd KMP MK42 ....29 G4
Willington Rd RBEDNE MK44..........23 G5
Willmers Cl BEDN MK41 ....13 G4
Willoughby Cl RBEDNE MK44.........16 D3
Willow Ri SDY/GAM/PO SG19..........27 F5
Willow Rd KMP MK42......................31 F1
The Willows AMP/FLIT/B * MK45....42 D4
RBEDW MK43.................................35 E1
Wilstead Hl AMP/FLIT/B MK45........43 H5
Wilstead Rd AMP/FLIT/B MK45 ......31 E5
AMP/FLIT/B MK45.........................38 C4
Winchester Rd KMP MK42 ....31 G2
SDY/GAM/PO SG19........................26 D2
The Windermere KMP MK42 ....29 H3
Windmill Cl BEDN MK41 ....14 B5
Windmill Hl BED MK40 ....19 H1
Windrush Av BEDN MK41 ....13 E3
Windsor Gdns BED MK40 ....21 F1
Windsor Rd KMP MK42....................31 F2
Windsor Wy SDY/GAM/PO SG19 ....27 E4
Wingfield Cl BED MK40...................20 A4
Wingfield Rd RBEDW MK43 ....10 D4
Winifred Rd BED MK40 ....20 B3
Witham Cl BEDN MK41 ....13 F1
Woburn Rd BED MK40 ....2 A3
KMP MK42 ....29 H4
RBEDW MK43.................................35 G1
RBEDW MK43.................................40 A5
Wolseley Rd RBEDW MK43.............29 H5
Wood Cl BED MK40 ....19 G2
Woodcock Cl
SDY/GAM/PO SG19........................26 D1
Woodcote BEDN MK41 ....13 H5
Wood End La RBEDW MK43...........28 C4
Wood End Rd RBEDW MK43...........28 B5
Woodfield La BEDN MK41 ....15 G3
Woodland Dr RBEDW MK43...........10 D4
Woodlands BEDN * MK41 ....12 D2
Woodlands Cl RBEDNE MK44.........33 G1
Wood La AMP/FLIT/B MK45 ....38 D2
BEDN MK41 ....15 E1
RBEDNE MK44 ....24 B4
Woodmere BEDN MK41 ....13 H5
Woodstock Rd BED MK40 ....20 B5
Woodville Dr BED MK40 ....19 F5
Woolfield SDY/GAM/PO SG19 ....27 F5
Wootton Rd RBEDW MK43.............28 D4
Wyatt Rd KMP MK42 ....29 H3
Wychwood Rd BEDN MK41 ....14 B5
Wye Cl BEDN MK41 ....13 F3
Wynnefield Wk
SDY/GAM/PO SG19........................27 E3

Y

Yeomans Ga RBEDNE MK44 ....32 D2
York St BED MK40 ....3 J3

Index - featured places

bey Middle School &
Swimming Pool
KMP MK42 .... 31 E3
e Acorn School
BED MK40 .... 21 E1
kwright Road
Industrial Estate
KMP MK42 .... 32 A1
spects Leisure Centre
BEDN MK41 .... 3 K5
illiol Lower School
KMP MK42 .... 29 H4
e Barns Hotel
RBEDNE MK44.............................. 22 B5
eauchamp Middle School
BEDN MK41 .... 12 D3
edford Athletic RUFC
BEDN MK41 .... 13 H3
edford Athletic Stadium
BEDN MK41 .... 21 H3
edford Business Centre
BED MK40 .... 3 F2
KMP MK42 .... 31 F2
edford Bus Station
BED MK40 .... 2 C3
edford College
BEDN MK41 .... 13 E5
KMP MK42 .... 30 A4
Bedford College of FE
KMP MK42 .... 2 D5
Bedford & County Golf Club
BEDN MK41 .... 12 B1
Bedford Cricket Club
BEDN MK41 .... 22 B1
The Bedford Golf Club
BED MK40 .... 19 E3
Bedford High School
BED MK40 .... 2 C2
Bedford Hospital
KMP MK42 .... 2 C7
Bedford Hospital (North Wing)
BED MK40 .... 3 F1
Bedford Lawn Tennis Club
BED MK40 .... 3 H1
Bedford Magistrates Court
KMP MK42 .... 2 D4
Bedford Modern School
BEDN MK41 .... 12 B5
Bedford Museum
BED MK40 .... 2 E3
Bedford Preparatory School
BED MK40 .... 2 E2
Bedford RUFC
BED MK40 .... 3 G1
Bedford Road Lower School
KMP MK42 .... 30 A2
Bedford Rowing Club
KMP MK42 .... 3 F4
Bedford School
BED MK40 .... 2 E1
Bedfordshire Golf Club
BED MK40 .... 19 H1
Bedford Town FC
RBEDNE MK44.............................. 22 D4
Biddenham Upper School
BED MK40 .... 19 H3
Bowen West Theatre
BED MK40 .... 2 A1
Bowling Alley
BEDN MK41 .... 3 K5
Brickhill Lower School
BEDN MK41 .... 13 F3
Broadmead Business Park
RBEDW MK43 .... 41 F2
Broadmead Lower School
RBEDW MK43 .... 41 G2
Bromham Mill & Art Gallery
RBEDW MK43 .... 18 D1
Bromham VC Lower School
RBEDW MK43 .... 10 D5
Building Research Establishment
RBEDNE MK44 .... 32 C4
Cambridge Road Industrial Estate
KMP MK42 .... 32 A1
Camestone Lower School
KMP MK42 .... 30 B2
Cardington Cross
RBEDNE MK44.............................. 32 C1
Castle Lower School
BED MK40 .... 3 H2
Castle Mound
BED MK40 .... 2 E4
Cauldwell Lower School
KMP MK42 .... 20 C5
Cecil Higgins Art Gallery
BED MK40 .... 2 E4
Church End Lower School
RBEDW MK43 .... 40 B5
Civic Theatre
BED MK40 .... 2 D4
Clapham Hospital
BEDN MK41 .... 5 G5
Community Hospitals
BED MK40 .... 2 C2
Cople Lower School
RBEDNE MK44.............................. 23 G5
Corn Exchange
BED MK40 .... 2 D3
Cotton End Lower School
AMP/FLIT/B MK45 .... 38 C1
Dame Alice Harpur School
KMP MK42 .... 3 F5

De Montfort University
BED MK40 .... **2** A1
BEDN MK41 .... **21** H1
De Parys Medical Centre
BED MK40 .... **2** E1
Edith Cavell Lower School
BEDN MK41 .... **20** C1
Elms Industrial Estate
BEDN MK41 .... **22** C1
Elstow Business Park
KMP MK42 .... **30** D1
Elstow Lower School
KMP MK42 .... **30** D2
Fenlake Road Industrial Estate
KMP MK42 .... **3** F7
Georgina Perkins School
BEDN MK41 .... **2** B1
Goldington Green Lower School
BEDN MK41 .... **22** B2
Goldington Middle School
BEDN MK41 .... **21** H1
Grange School
KMP MK42 .... **30** A1
Great Barford Lower School
RBEDNE MK44 .... **16** D3
Harpur Music School
BED MK40 .... **2** B1
Harrowden Middle School
KMP MK42 .... **31** G1
Hastingsbury Upper School
KMP MK42 .... **29** G4
Hazeldene Lower School
BEDN MK41 .... **13** G5
The Hills Lower School
BEDN MK41 .... **13** G5
HM Prison
BED MK40 .... **2** D2
Houghton Conquest Lower School
AMP/FLIT/B MK45 .... **42** D4
Innkeeper's Lodge
BEDN MK41 .... **22** B1
Interchange Retail Park
AMP/FLIT/B MK45 .... **30** B4
John Bunyan Museum
BED MK40 .... **2** E3
John Bunyan Upper School
KMP MK42 .... **31** G2
Kempston Mill Industrial Estate
BED MK40 .... **29** G2
Kempston Rural Lower School
RBEDW MK43 .... **29** F2
Kempston Swimming Pool
KMP MK42 .... **20** B5
Laburnum Lower School
SDY/GAM/PO SG19 .... **26** D4
Lansdowne Road Surgery
BED MK40 .... **2** B2
Lincroft Middle School
RBEDW MK43 .... **11** E1
Livingstone Lower School
BEDN MK41 .... **20** C1
London Road Health Centre
KMP MK42 .... **21** F5
Manor Hospital
BED MK40 .... **19** F3
Mark Rutherford School
BEDN MK41 .... **14** A3
Marlborough Lower School
BED MK40 .... **20** A3
Marlowes Health Centre
BED MK40 .... **2** C1
Marsh Leys Industrial Estate
RBEDW MK43 .... **35** H1
Marston Vale Middle School
RBEDW MK43 .... **41** F3
Midland Structures Industrial Estate
KMP MK42 .... **30** C1
Moggerhanger Lower School
RBEDNE MK44 .... **25** G4
Moot Hall
KMP MK42 .... **30** D2
Mowsbury Golf Club
BEDN MK41 .... **13** G1
Newnham Middle School
BED MK40 .... **21** F1
Oasis Swimming Pool
KMP MK42 .... **3** K6
Pavenham Park Golf Course
RBEDW MK43 .... **4** B1
Polam School
BED MK40 .... **2** A1
Post Mill
RBEDW MK43 .... **10** A2
Priory Business Park
RBEDNE MK44 .... **22** C4
Priory Country Park
RBEDNE MK44 .... **22** A4
Priory Lower School
BED MK40 .... **2** B3
Putnoe Lower School
BEDN MK41 .... **13** H5
Queens Park Lower School
BED MK40 .... **20** A3
Rainbow Special School
RBEDW MK43 .... **10** A5
Ravensden Lower School
RBEDNE MK44 .... **8** B4
Renhold CE Lower School
BEDN MK41 .... **14** D2
The Ridgeway Business Park
RBEDNE MK44 .... **26** A3
Ridgeway Special School
KMP MK42 .... **29** G4
Riverside Lawn Tennis Club
BED MK40 .... **3** J1
Robert Bruce Middle School
KMP MK42 .... **29** H2
Robert Peel Lower School
SDY/GAM/PO SG19 .... **27** E3
Robinson Pool
BEDN MK41 .... **20** D1
RSPB Headquarters & Reserve
SDY/GAM/PO SG19 .... **27** H5
Rushmoor School
BED MK40 .... **20** B1
St Andrews School
BED MK40 .... **21** E1
St Bedes Middle School
BED MK40 .... **2** A2
St Gregorys Middle School
BED MK40 .... **20** A2
St James Lower School
BED MK40 .... **19** F2
St John Rigby Lower School
BED MK40 .... **21** G1
St Johns Special School
KMP MK42 .... **20** B5
St Josephs Lower School
BED MK40 .... **20** A3
St Martins Business Centre
KMP MK42 .... **32** A1
St Thomas More Catholic School
BEDN MK41 .... **12** D2
Sandy Business Park
SDY/GAM/PO SG19 .... **27** E1
Sandy Health Centre
SDY/GAM/PO SG19 .... **27** E4
Sandy Place Middle School
SDY/GAM/PO SG19 .... **27** E5
Sandy Upper School & Community College
SDY/GAM/PO SG19 .... **27** E2
Scott Lower School
BEDN MK41 .... **12** D3
Sedgemoor College
BED MK40 .... **20** B1
Shackleton Lower School
KMP MK42 .... **21**
Shelton Lower School
RBEDW MK43 .... **40**
Shortstown Lower School
KMP MK42 .... **31**
Springfield Lower School
KMP MK42 .... **30**
Star Rowing Club
BED MK40 .... **2**
Stephenson Lower School
KMP MK42 .... **31**
Stewartby Lake Country Park
RBEDW MK43 .... **40**
Travel Inn
RBEDNE MK44 .... **21**
UGC Cimema
BEDN MK41 .... **3**
Union Street Clinic
BED MK40 .... **2**
Ursula Taylor Lower School
BEDN MK41 .... **12**
Viking Industrial Estate
BEDN MK41 .... **14**
Walmsley House School
BED MK40 .... **21**
Westfield Middle School
BED MK40 .... **20**
Wilden Va Lower School
RBEDNE MK44 .... **9**
Willington Lower School
RBEDNE MK44 .... **24**
Wilstead Industrial Park
AMP/FLIT/B MK45 .... **36**
Wilstead Lower School
AMP/FLIT/B MK45 .... **43**
Woburn Road Industrial Estate
KMP MK42 .... **30**
Wolseley Business Park
RBEDW MK43 .... **30**
Woodlands Manor Hotel
BEDN MK41 .... **12**
Woodside Middle School
BEDN MK41 .... **14**
Wootton Lower School
RBEDW MK43 .... **34**
Wootton Upper School
RBEDW MK43 .... **34**

Acknowledgements

The Post Office is a registered trademark of Post Office Ltd. in the UK and other countries.

Schools address data provided by Education Direct.

Petrol station information supplied by Johnsons

One-way street data provided by © Tele Atlas N.V. Tele Atlas

Garden centre information provided b

Garden Centre Association Britains best garden centr

Wyevale Garden Centr

QUESTIONNAIRE

Dear Atlas User
Your comments, opinions and recommendations are very important to us. So please help us to improve our street atlases by taking a few minutes to complete this simple questionnaire.

You do NOT need a stamp (unless posted outside the UK). If you do not want to remove this page from your street atlas, then photocopy it or write your answers on a plain sheet of paper.

Send to: The Editor, AA Street by Street, FREEPOST SCE 4598, Basingstoke RG21 4GY

ABOUT THE ATLAS...

Which city/town/county did you buy?

Are there any features of the atlas or mapping that you find particularly useful?

Is there anything we could have done better?

Why did you choose an AA Street by Street atlas?

Did it meet your expectations?

Exceeded ☐ **Met all** ☐ **Met most** ☐ **Fell below** ☐

Please give your reasons

ML106z

continued overleaf

Where did you buy it?

For what purpose? (please tick all applicable)

To use in your own local area ☐ **To use on business or at work** ☐

Visiting a strange place ☐ **In the car** ☐ **On foot** ☐

Other (please state)

LOCAL KNOWLEDGE...

Local knowledge is invaluable. Whilst every attempt has been made to make the information contained in this atlas as accurate as possible, should you notice any inaccuracies, please detail them below (if necessary, use a blank piece of paper) or e-mail us at *streetbystreet@theAA.com*

ABOUT YOU...

Name (Mr/Mrs/Ms)

Address

Postcode

Daytime tel no

E-mail address

Which age group are you in?

Under 25 ☐ **25-34** ☐ **35-44** ☐ **45-54** ☐ **55-64** ☐ **65+** ☐

Are you an AA member? **YES** ☐ **NO** ☐

Do you have Internet access? **YES** ☐ **NO** ☐

Thank you for taking the time to complete this questionnaire. Please send it to us as soon as possible, and remember, you do not need a stamp (unless posted outside the UK).

ML